The Little
Boy in Me

The Little
Boy in Me

George G. Bloomer

THE LITTLE BOY IN ME by George G. Bloomer
Published by Creation House Press
A part of Strang Communications Company
600 Rinehart Road
Lake Mary, Florida 32746
www.creationhouse.com

Unless otherwise noted, all Scripture quotations are from the King James Version of the Bible.

Scripture quotations marked NKJV are from the New King James Version of the Bible. Copyright © 1979, 1980, 1982 by Thomas Nelson, Inc., publishers. Used by permission.

Library of Congress Card Number: 00-106781
ISBN: 0-88419-750-6 (paperback)

01234567 *** 87654321
Printed in the United States of America

Dedication

I dedicate this book to the Bethel Family Worship Center, Steadfast and Unmovable Men's Ministry and to my dearest friend and son in the Gospel, Darren Meadows—who has become a man before my eyes and has left sonship and begun fathering.

I dedicate this book also to the Bethel Family Worship Center young men's fellowship, M.O.B. (Men of Bethel).

I also dedicate this book to the women's ministry, Women Professing Godliness—may this book serve as an excellent guide for discerning your eternal soul mate.

Acknowledgements

To my wife Jeanie Bloomer and my two daughters Jessica and Jennifer Bloomer—I want you to know how much I love you and appreciate you. To my staff at Blooming House, Kimberly Meadows, Sharon King, and Stacy Johnson, thank you for your assistance and dedication in completing this project.

Contents

Introduction

A man who refuses to grow up is in essence attempting to defy the laws of nature. His body takes on the physical appearance of a full grown male, yet his attitudes and actions are those of a child. He simply shows no desire to mature mentally, emotionally and spiritually. To the casual observer, he seems like a normal guy. And unless the observer has keen insight and can discern spirits, this fellow will simply appear to be happy-go-lucky and enjoying life to its fullest. Yet inwardly, this "man-boy" is a ball of confusion and turmoil. His fake laughter and artificial joy are a facade to hide his insecurity and fear. Yet, the solution to his problem is the very thing he fears the most—

growth. As a result, this little boy first becomes a young man trapped between the carefree bliss of youth and the harsh realities of adulthood. He then becomes an older man who has spent the majority of his life trying to defy the inevitable. This has happened and is still happening to too many men. That is why it is very important that we learn to identify this tendency in a child in order to defeat this demonic spirit at a young age. This behavior has no social, economic or ethnic prejudice; it crosses all walks of life, races and creeds. Many times there is nothing outwardly bizarre or unusual about these men, especially the younger men, because we have become conditioned to expect no more from them than immature, "youthful" behavior. However, the Spirit of Christ enables us to recognize the danger of this behavior–evolving from the "norm" to the questionable to the totally unacceptable. These men are extremely relaxed in their responsibilities and prefer "cover-ups" as opposed to accountability. While most of us begin the process of growing out of this behavior once we leave childhood and merge into adolescence, some men simply refuse to make the transfer...thus, the reason for this book. For too long, mature adults have ignored or sanctioned those who never wanted to grow up. But those who are strong must minister to those who are weak. This text will help you understand why your son, husband, or long-time friend behaves the way he does. Does his behavior not reflect his age? Is he a likeable person, but there is that "one thing" about him that gets on your last nerve? Well, let's find out why. Read on and be blessed and perhaps even equipped to help set someone free!

—PASTOR GEORGE BLOOMER

Part 1

The Abused Boy

*The Devil Thought He
Had Me, But I Got Away*

1

A Man Before My Time

"My Testimony"

*I*t was July of 1976. A series of events took place that year that not only made history for the nation, but also shaped my future. America celebrated its bicentennial, the president during this time was Gerald R. Ford, and I became a man—or so it seemed. At the age of twelve I became a man and, at the same time, my innocence was robbed from me. Let's take a trip into the past as I explain the events that led up to my instant growth.

I remember my address so clearly: 453 Columbia Street, Brooklyn, New York, zip code 11213, apartments A, B, and C. My mother had nine children by my father, and it was said that my father had fifteen other children by six other women in the same project

1

area where I grew up. Although all of the fifteen other children have not been confirmed, whether more or less, we all knew that there were other children.

Summer days were hot—scorching hot, as we would say in South Brooklyn—where I grew up in a community called Red Hook. To keep cool, we'd open the fire hydrant as the temperature would rise to the high nineties and sometimes peak at one hundred. Our days were filled with playing in the fire hydrant, going to the community pool to keep cool, building go-carts for neighborhood races, playing "scalzies" (a home-made game you played by filling bottle caps with tar and flicking them into a box), kick the can, hide the bacon, and tag. It's important for you to understand that I grew up in poverty and was raised on welfare. We were poverty stricken, to say the least.

CONTENTMENT IN LACK

My mother had nine children, and public housing provided us three apartments, which in retrospect I refer to as the *penthouse in the projects—a condo in the ghetto.* My mother received $500 per month in food stamps, a welfare check of $385 twice a month on the first and fifteenth of each month, and a Medicaid card periodically. A government surplus truck would come and issue food in the community. This food consisted of peanut butter, powdered eggs, powdered milk, corn meal, flour, canned pork, canned chicken, and canned lunch meat, which many people refer to now as Spam.

As you can see, we grew up very poor with limited resources, but I did not know or realize these limitations at the time. I thought I was just as normal as anyone else and as rich and fortunate as others, too. I had no idea that the food shortages we experienced, which sometimes lasted for two or three days before the next check would come, were a nonstandard way of life. I thought everyone experienced this hunger and lifestyle of lack.

I had no idea—I *really* had no idea—that we were poor. I was taught to learn to do without, feel good about it, and expect *nothing* so that I could never be disappointed for not having the things I desired. I learned contentment in lack. I would later carry these experiences with me into adulthood—man on the outside, little boy within.

THE PARTY, THE ROOM, THE FIGHT

This is where I would like to begin telling you my story. Her name was Peggy* and I was eleven and a half years old. She was twenty-nine. She had a boyfriend, whom I now know was her live-in lover. I came to know her through running errands for her. She was a friend of the family, a partying friend of my mother's. I would see her at the apartment every weekend when my mother's friends would come over to drink, cuss, and play cards. But Ms. Peggy was always very nice to me. She had three children—Arthur, Jasper, and Wendy. As I look back and remember, I can recall very clearly how much Ms. Peggy really loved and protected those children. Arthur was one year younger than me; Jasper was three years younger; and the daughter, Wendy, was five years younger.

One night a number of adults gathered at my mother's apartment as usual. There was always "booze," cigarette smoke, an empty refrigerator,

*not her real name

filled ashtrays, and beer cans and bottles in the trash, hungry children and intoxicated parents. No matter what the situation, no matter how rough things got, there was always a way to get alcohol. I remember that.

One night after the crowd had gathered, the music was playing, chicken was frying, and the card game was in full swing. But suddenly an argument broke out. Peggy had walked in a room and caught her "man" in bed with one of her girlfriends. Right in the house under all of our noses, while everyone else was preoccupied, "Mack-Daddy" had slipped off with Peggy's girlfriend to engage in sexual acts in one of the rooms of our house. My mother was infuriated.

"In my house!" she screamed. "In my @#*! house! How could you do this?" she continued shouting. Then Peggy began yelling. She ran into the kitchen, grabbed a butcher knife and started swinging at him. Now remember, during this time I'm a little boy, eleven and a half years old, and I'm seeing all of this, but I don't fully understand it. I don't understand my mother being upset or even Ms. Peggy. Why didn't I understand? Because it was me, "little ol' me," who hid under the same bed, in the same room, on a number of Friday nights and witnessed everyone being unfaithful to each other—Ms. Peggy included! When there was food in the house and a card game going on, it was normal for me and a friend, or one of my brothers, to hide under the bed and eat chicken, unbeknownst to the different ones who would enter the bedroom and engage in sexual activities above us. We did not understand the sexual experience completely, but we did know that something was wrong with these sexual acts.

THE BOY BECOMES A "MAN"

Needless to say, the relationship between Ms. Peggy and her boyfriend was now over. A few days later, or perhaps a few weeks, I was asked to run an errand for Ms. Peggy. She would always treat me so nice. Now that her boyfriend was gone, she would call on me more often—occasionally three times within a day. I noticed that she would hug me, pay me, and then kiss me on my cheek. But I noticed that the kisses were getting closer and closer to my lips. Then one afternoon it all began. The twenty-nine-year-old woman introduced the now twelve-year-old boy to the world of adult sexuality.

Yes, for the next few months I would become the victim of Ms. Peggy's molestation and perversion. I would continue to visit her home on several different occasions as she taught me her version of love, and I learned about sex as seen through the eyes of Ms. Peggy. I thought of this behavior as a bit strange at first, but I also began to grow more and more fond of her. She was my first, and in my eyes, I was her one and only. Soon, however, this outlook would change and reality would set in.

On my way to her apartment one day, I looked up and there on the balcony was Ms. Peggy, but she was not alone. Instead she was engaged in a very intimate embrace with a man about her same age—her new love—the man who would now take my place and fill the void of loneliness in Ms. Peggy's life. I was crushed! *How could she do this to me?* I thought, standing there weeping, knowing that I would no longer be the man in her life because another man—a real man—had come to take my place. How could I compete? I decided not to even try. So I ran away and continued my childhood games of marbles and tag. It was now over!

As I grew older I realized that this experience, accompanied by other encounters, created a hiding place for the little boy trapped inside the body of a full-grown man. Many other encounters happened in my life after this incident that also threatened to abort my destiny and affect my view on relationships. I now know, however, that it is only the grace of God that has allowed me to treat others not as I was treated, but with caution, gentleness, and meekness.

THE BIRTH OF A CHURCH—THE BIRTH OF A MAN

During the birth of the church that I currently pastor, I discovered firsthand this *hidden boy* trapped in the bodies of men. As wives complained during counseling sessions about their husbands' neglect of responsibility, I began to question what was the root cause for this behavior. Although these men gave a first impression of being responsible and mature full-grown men, inwardly they were little boys who had no regard for husbandry or fatherly duties. From neglect to laziness, lying, and, in extreme cases, physical abuse, this behavior was inexcusable. But even I, one from a broken home myself, had to admit that this behavior was not only inexcusable but also intolerable. I was so bothered by the testimonies of these women who had endured this treatment for so many years prior to even joining the church that some nights I even lost sleep over it. It would be months later that I would find out why my grief ran so deep. You see, I too, in part, had been a victim of this *little boy syndrome*.

I'd been in ministry for about fourteen years when one day I finally returned to preach in the Red Hook Projects in Brooklyn, New York, where I had grown up. Hundreds came out to see George Bloomer, whom they still saw in their minds as a little boy running around Red Hook projects who had somehow managed to escape the clutches of project living. Here in the neighborhood of my past I was the preacher—though I had been the one least likely to escape the trap of poverty and lawlessness, much less minister the Word of the Lord. Wow! But I guess seeing was believing. I ministered three nights, and, after concluding the service on the final night, I was greeted by an older woman.

"Hi, George," she said.

Unable to recognize her, I felt puzzled but returned her greeting with a warm, "Hi, how are you?" Realizing that I had no idea who she was, she revealed herself.

"Remember me? I'm Tara's mother."

As my memory drifted back to my childhood days, I finally recognized this woman as one who had publicly humiliated me in front of my peers for talking to her daughter, Tara. It felt as if I was suddenly taken out of the present and into my past, and I could hear this lady screaming at me, "I don't ever want to see you talking to my daughter again!" She had screamed at my terrified eleven-year-old figure standing before her with humiliation to make her point as clear as day. "You're no good, your family is no good, and nothing good is ever going to come out of you!" I could hear those words from my past being echoed as clear that day as if it were happening all over again. When I came to myself, I found that because I was now converted, I was able to lay aside that anger and humiliation and greet her sincerely. "So, how is Tara?" I asked.

"Well, George, Tara isn't well," she responded. "She has AIDS and two of her babies are crack babies." I was stunned beyond what mere words could say. As she turned to walk away she took a few steps and turned back to say, "I sure do wish things could have worked out between you and Tara."

It was at that moment that I realized I had been carrying oppressive weights from my childhood and young adult years for years, and I didn't even know it. Instantly, a weight dropped off, and later I realized that I no longer felt the low self-esteem that caused me to feel incapable of handling the call of God upon my life. The little eleven-year-old boy who had been hiding inside of me suddenly grew up to match the full-grown man on the outside. No longer was I a boy trapped inside a man's body, but I began to experience adulthood in its purest and most sincere form. God had used the same woman who once oppressed me to now meet up with me again and speak the words to set me free! I was finally delivered! It was my deliverance that now allows me to better understand the hindrances that many men face in dealing with some of the same experiences from their childhoods.

WE ALL KNOW HIM

Picture for a moment, if you will, a young man between the ages of thirty and thirty-five, from a middle-class background, and, at first-glance, an extremely likable and approachable person, and indeed very charming. We will call him Jonathan.

Your first impression of Jonathan is that of a young man who, by all accounts, has it all together, full of happiness and excitement, pursuing life with unflinching vigor. For the sake of this example, assume that you are a young lady, and you and Jonathan start to date. As the relationship progresses, however, you notice Jonathan's lack of responsibility and carefree attitude about routine adult tasks. He chooses inopportune times to "flaunt his stuff," and, as it relates to women, he tends to put his foot in his mouth.

Now, equipped with this new information, you ask yourself. *Why do I even put up with this guy?* Why? Because in spite of his weaknesses, Jonathan is a very nice guy, maybe a little misguided, but he does mean well. Or maybe you tell yourself, *I'm the only "true" friend he has; if I cut Jonathan off at this point, what's going to happen to him?* So you continue to endure the torment, the anger, the embarrassment, comforting yourself with the notion that this guy just simply does not know any better. Well, perhaps you're right. This guy may not know any better. But why? And who is he? He is a physically full-grown male who stopped growing emotionally and intellectually at adolescence. Therefore, the full-grown thirty-year-old male, whom you think you see, is really a twelve-year-old boy trapped in the body of a man. Not only does he not know how to get out, but, unfortunately, he is totally unaware that he *needs* to get out.

Immediately, we who are Christians think, *Well, this man needs salvation.* But the church is filled to capacity with tongue-talking, Holy-Ghost-filled, converted little boys hiding in the bodies of grown men. They may even cast out demons in Jesus' name, but when the anointing lifts, that same bravery and maturity may cease to exist. Paul said in 1 Corinthians 9:27: "I keep under my body and bring it into subjection: lest that by any means, when I have preached to others, I myself should be a castaway."

We must confront this epidemic in order to free ourselves from its results. Immature men can serve as the major catalyst in the destruction of relationships, without either of the two parties ever discovering the root cause of the void in the relationship. Mothers experience it with sons, sons with fathers, wives with husbands, sisters with their brothers, and so on. The question then becomes, where does this behavior originate? It normally starts at adolescence and either wears off or develops into more serious psychological problems, thus preventing anything but dysfunctional relationships throughout this man's life. When his permissiveness and irresponsible attitude go unchallenged, he further slides into the illusion of his own perfection and chauvinistic outlook on life.

PARENTAL GUIDANCE AND PREVENTION

As a parent, it is not always a good idea to suffer in silence when family problems arise. Children will sense that something is wrong and begin to blame themselves, which will eventually stunt their emotional growth by holding on to things that they are too young to handle or understand. Neither is it a good idea to avoid family conflict by brushing children off with idle words of comfort that mean absolutely nothing. Children tend to view this as rejection, developing complexes about themselves and taking out their frustration on others.

This type of behavior spills over into adulthood. Many times this is where we see grown men acting like children when things just don't go their way. Trying to fill the void in a child's life with excuses, false promises, money, and other materialistic gifts is no substitute for time. Quality time means sitting down with children and confronting issues that may at times create a bit of discomfort for both parties involved; nonetheless, when problems arise they must be addressed. Confrontation is a very important ingredient in the growth process.

Remember that Satan sends natural occurrences to frustrate you spiritually to get you to abort your spiritual destiny. Don't allow the destiny of your home to be aborted by natural occurrences. Regardless of the situation and circumstances, there is always made a way of escape.

Satan worked hard during my childhood to create circumstances that would lead me to abort my spiritual destiny. But God showed me that if his tactics can be uncovered and attacked spiritually, then I could learn to become the man God destined me to become. In the next chapter I will identify the behavior of the little boy within and show you how to change his ways through the power of words.

2

The Truth Revealed

*T*he little boy inside the body of a man has indeed touched and, in extreme cases, destroyed the lives of many. His character develops at a very young age, and if not noticed or steered in the proper direction, his immature behavior becomes a nuisance to all who encounter him as an adult. If we take a brief moment to reflect on some of our past, or perhaps present, male encounters, we will realize that we have all, at one time or another, met this "adult-boy." But maybe now we can become better equipped to understand, and with God's help, also steer him in the right direction.

The Little Boy in Me

THE WARNING SIGNS

His personality and character are revealed in various forms. During his adolescent years he may show severe signs of impatience, wanting everything right now—refusing to listen to reason. He displays a lack of responsibility and is quick to point the finger at others for his own undisciplined actions, which is a sure sign of disobedience, no matter how subtle or overt the finger-pointing or actions may be. A word of caution: during this crucial time and along with these signs, this teenage male may only show signs of true happiness when surrounded by his peers. Many times this is a sign of loneliness.

But what's even more dangerous is the open door in the form of loneliness that Satan uses to bring about peer pressure—causing the teen to engage in activities that he normally would not indulge in away from his peers: drugs, alcohol, sexual perversion, theft, and lawlessness, to name a few. If the behavior is not addressed at this level, as the male teen approaches age eighteen and enters into adulthood, his ego begins to play out his immaturity and lack of growth through a chauvinistic personality. Finally, once he reaches his late twenties to early thirties, this chauvinistic way of thinking clouds his outlook on life. It's all about *him*, and he mistakenly thinks that the world owes him something.

THE DEBT HAS BEEN PAID

How do I know this? Because I too was one who once felt that the world owed me something. Growing up in poverty and being reared through the welfare system, I felt that society owed me something for all the "hell" I had to endure due to my poverty-stricken environment as a child. Nonetheless, I quickly learned the principle of Matthew 11:12: "the kingdom of heaven suffereth violence, and the violent take it by force." Of course, this does not mean physical force or starting a riot but simply making up in your mind that although God has a plan for your life, you determine the death or life of that destiny by choosing either small-minded thinking or faith in God to perform the impossible. Jesus Christ has already paid the debt for us; now it's up to us to seize the inheritance.

I realized that if I was ever going to do great exploits for the Lord, leave an inheritance for my children, become a good spouse, and all the other responsibilities that go along with being a man, then I would have to take great leaps of faith. I learned to trust in God and to give before expecting to receive. I knew that I simply needed to have the mind of Christ, to put my hands to the plow, and not to look back.

Likewise, if you are a man and find yourself being outlined within the pages of this text, you need to understand that it's not too late for you to turn your life around and receive deliverance and a new direction for life.

We must realize that this is a universal problem with no ethnic or social barriers. Every neighborhood, no matter how poor or affluent it may be, has an "adult-boy" whom they can point out with no hesitation. That is why we must not allow pride to become the barrier that hinders us from receiving our deliverance. Hebrews 12:1 says that we are to "lay aside *every* weight, and the sin which doth so easily beset us, and let us run with patience the race that is set before us" (italics added). Pride is a weight, and the refusal of man to lay aside this weight is the sin that so easily, and unnecessarily, besets him. Pride prevents the deliverance and stunts the growth of so many men who have the right to be set free!

She Desires Protection, Too

In most cases, this person is a "nice guy" but very misguided. He tends to not be very independent, and, if he has a wife, she complains of his lack of stability and dependence on her and others. The wife may find herself giving and giving to this man—making daily deposits with no interest earned or returns made on her investments, while he continues to make withdrawals. She becomes tired and may finally decide that it is easier to give in to or expect this behavior rather than expect more from him. Therefore, she becomes mother and wife, in that order, as opposed to being his helpmeet as the Bible ordains. And, if she is a woman who simply decides she cannot tolerate this behavior any longer, the marriage is filled with tension. Arguments break out over things that have absolutely nothing to do with the heart of the matter, which is the little boy whose mental and emotional growth has been stunted.

For instance, what she really feels is that he should be more protective of her, be more responsible, give her the same attention that she gives to him or to sum it all up...to just grow up! But because he has never really been challenged as it relates to his behavior, he feels that she is just being unreasonable and "makes a big deal out of everything." So, when he chastises the son or daughter of the family with a statement like, "Act your age," she runs to the rescue of the child because in her mind she's saying, "Practice what you preach!" Meanwhile, he is totally clueless and has no idea why she is "overreacting."

What's the end result? Typically these two people spend years living in misery or eventually divorce. The two usually never deal with the root of the matter—a little boy trapped in the body of grown man who was probably never properly fathered himself. Or maybe he is simply accustomed to having things handed to him on a silver platter.

TAKING OFF THE MASK

Some immature men remain single but they are not attracted to women their age or older. They steer more toward women who are younger than they are and less experienced in life. I often joke with the women in my church that the potential wives for whom these men are searching are located somewhere on Mars. This is because most of these men want a flawless woman while they, by all accounts, fail in perfection themselves.

I say all of this not to promote negativity upon the men, but only to share with others from what I have been delivered and from what I have seen other men delivered by the power of God as well. For too long Satan has had his way in the growth process of men, who are supposed to be the first partakers of the fruit. He must be exposed for who he is in order for the growth process to begin and for men to take their rightful place in the home, in the body of

The Little Boy in Me

Christ, and in society as a whole. We are "destroyed for a lack of knowledge" (Hos. 4:6). In order to stop this needless destruction, then, knowledge must be increased.

Knowledge is a weapon against ignorance and inferiority. Because many of the victims of this little-boy syndrome never reach their highest potential, they become very dissatisfied with the void in their life. They stray from one project to the next, never completing one thing, because they don't take time to develop a plan or a strategy on how to conquer and overcome the giants in their lives. They are unstable and double-minded.

I once knew a young man whom we'll call Wade. After I had spent time training and pouring spiritual and basic principles into this young man, he was forced to make a startling discovery about himself. He'd spent several years in a façade of male adulthood and egotistical authority, only to realize that even with all of his education and natural abilities, he was still a little boy trapped inside the body of a man. For years people had patted him on his back and encouraged his immaturity, while his life and family were literally falling apart before his very eyes.

Now, some may expect me to say that I should have laid hands on him, anointed him with oil and cast this spirit out. I did quite the contrary. As the Holy Spirit began to reveal to me his underlying problems and his negligence to address those problems, I simply told this young man the truth. Of course, there was also prayer involved, but, most importantly, God set him free by me simply telling this young man the truth about himself.

As I sat him down and shared with him a number

of things that the Lord had revealed to me concerning the little boy on the inside of him and matters that he refused to address, he broke down. Through his sobbing he admitted that he was tired of living the lie and being placed on a pedestal upon which he was not ready, nor properly equipped, to stand. Indeed God had His hands upon this young man's life, but because prior leaders had chosen to use him, pervert his gift, and not tell him the truth, the little boy on the inside of him had become too arrogant and stubborn to admit that a growth process was needed. He was now, however, ready to be set free.

Over the next few months I witnessed a true transformation take place in his life that not only took him to another level spiritually and financially, but also saved his family and marriage. Today his testimony is, "When I was child, I spake as a child, I understood as a child, I thought as a child: but when I became a man, I put away childish things" (1 Cor. 13:11).

WORDS THE KEYS TO YOUR DESTINY

In the chapter entitled "A Man Before My Time," I shared with you how I grew up in poverty but didn't know it. The Bible teaches us that life and death are in the power of the tongue. I was ignorant of my poverty-stricken situation because no life was being articulated to me. You see, everyone around me was in the same situation—an illusion, if you will, a dream—*no, a nightmare*. Having the power to speak life, instead they spoke death and didn't know it.

The worst thing a person can do is to live in the

reality of another person's opinion—to be boxed in, limited, made to believe that this is what life has to offer and you have to accept it. "This is the hand that you were dealt, so stop bellyaching and deal with it," you begin telling yourself. No one is there to tell you that you can change your life, so you buy into the lie. But remember, no matter how many times you lose in life, always keep winning on your mind. Be determined to change and see it through. In viewing the lives of once-failed individuals who are now living successfully, you will see how words full of life were the keys that helped them to achieve their destiny.

My words of life came from a woman who moved into the projects shortly after I started taking drugs. I had a $200- to $300-per-day cocaine addiction and lived in a world of imagination and hallucinations. At this point in my life, God released words of life in the form of an "angel" in her late fifties who had a deep spiritual conviction and powerful revelation of the Lord. Unbeknownst to her, the words she spoke would change and govern my life. She would teach me things that I thought I knew and introduce me to the world outside of Red Hook projects. This new exposure would open up a whole new way of thinking and insight for me regarding life. Things that most people took for granted, I was just beginning to experience and learn about. For instance, I thought I knew what a daisy was, but I didn't. I had instead been exposed to a field of only dandelions—weeds—and thought they were valuable plants—that is, until I met this woman who exposed me to a world that I had no idea even existed.

I'd been living in an illusion, my own reality, and

I was learning that my own world was the exception and not the rule. But now my appetite to learn was beginning to change. The hunger pains increased as I desired to know more and more about what the real world had to offer. As knowledge increased, however, so did my frustration—desiring to go to the next level yet lacking the understanding of how to do so. But this lady, Ms. Ringle, had taught me that there was more to life than my illusion, more to life than the confines of Red Hook. Although Ms. Ringle never moved outside of Red Hook after that, she was content to make sure that both her children did. They were both college students at the time, and I was able to accompany Ms. Ringle to some of their college functions and finally their graduations.

It was during these functions that I was exposed to the lifestyles of others whom I'd never fellow-shipped with before, and she experienced the pleasure of pouring into someone else's life while seeing her children prosper as well. Although it would be years later before I actually walked into what God had stored up for me, the important thing was that the seed had been planted.

Without a seed there is no growth. So many times men use the giants in their lives as excuses for their lack of growth. Even with the seed planted, it must be nurtured and cared for by the right caretakers. It must be watered with words of life. Words can bring life, but the wrong words can kill.

You must be the one who takes the initiative to excel beyond the hindrances and go to that next level. Hindrances become like tight shoes on a baby's feet, preventing growth. Be careful what you allow people to speak into your spirit. The Bible says that life and death are in the power of the tongue (Prov. 18:21). But whose tongue? Life and death are in the power of *your* tongue (see v. 20). Therefore, no one else can determine your destiny. It's what you say about yourself that matters, not what your neighbor says about you. Only *you* hold the key to whether or not you go to that next level. It's your decision.

In this chapter we've learned that truth is one of the best things you can do to stop little-boy syndrome. Instead of making excuses, acknowledge your own shortcomings and look at their source in your past. Then make the decision to change your destiny by seeking out words of life.

In the next chapter you will learn how to take on positions of leadership and authority.

3

Little Boys in Big Positions

*P*lacing little boys in big positions can sometimes lead to great disasters. It's very important to seek the face of God about His timing when it comes to position because it's not the title of a position that makes it so important, but it is the responsibility that comes along with that title. Placing yourself in a position that you know you are not yet capable nor equipped to handle not only hinders your growth, but it also hinders the growth of those who have been placed under your supervision. That is not to say that we should be fearful of stepping out in faith when God has called us. However, at the same time we should be sure of the timing of God, His direction and plan for our lives.

Part of becoming a well-developed man both spiritually and naturally is being able to first receive instruction from others, such as pastors, supervisors, or other leaders who have been placed over him to help aid in the growth process. Of course, this principle pertains to women as well, but in this chapter we speak concerning men, especially since men, because of their natural-born egos, oftentimes find it insulting for others to instruct them in the right direction or to speak into their lives. The common response is usually, "I'm a man...I know what I'm doing...I don't need anyone trying to tell me what to do... I have it all under control!"

WHEN ZEAL RUNS OUT

A young, newly converted brother joined the church and was very excited about the things of God. I knew he desired to preach, and I could see that in his heart he felt he was ready. As his pastor and the one that God had ordained to speak into his life, I also knew that I had to be honest with him concerning what the Lord had shown me about his enthusiasm to move forth. I had to tell him the truth. So I did. "Thomas, you are full of zeal and enthusiasm concerning the things of the Lord," I began to explain. "But when the zeal runs out, you must have some experiences and knowledge in order to make it. Now, what I would like for you to do is to not be so quick to rush into ministry. You need to first allow me to teach you so that you can learn the voice of God for yourself and be able to stand when the attacks of the enemy and hard times come," I concluded.

Well, not only was Thomas not ready for ministry, but he was also not ready or willing to listen to what I had to say. He felt that I was only trying to hold him back, so Thomas left the church. He rushed into ministry at another church where he suddenly found out that everything I had told him in love was exactly what he needed to hear.

Upon finding out about Thomas's lack of knowledge concerning the Word of the Lord and his refusal to listen to reasoning, the other church he had now joined rebuked him openly and asked him to leave. Where would Thomas be today if he had simply listened and allowed the Word of the Lord to be his guide? Indeed, it is hard to say, but certainly he'd be a lot further along in his walk with the Lord and his spiritual destiny.

Think for a moment. How many times have you ignored the voice of reasoning that was speaking into your life only because you wanted to prove that you could do it or because you were full of the zeal without godly experiences to back you up?

DARE TO CONFRONT YOUR GOLIATH

Well, God wants to change your zeal into your testimony. There are numerous accounts of great men in the Bible who humbled themselves long enough to receive the call of God upon their lives. Let's take a peek into the life of David for a moment. In 1 Samuel 17 we see David, a young boy who believed in God enough to confront the giant Goliath. When the mockers scorned him, David did not stand there and argue with them about how wrong they were. Instead, David turned away from them and went straight to Saul and said, "Let no

25

man's heart fail because of him; thy servant will go and fight with this Philistine" (1 Sam. 17:32). Saul doubted and said to David, "Thou art but a youth, and he a man of war from his youth" (v. 33). Saul focused on David's age and size, thus discrediting David's ability to take upon himself such a great task. But the little boy, David, had great faith in God, and the Lord's anointing was upon this boy's life.

We see this same scenario play out amongst us today. God is beginning to appoint young boys with great faith to do the job of grown men who are too afraid and lack the faith to carry out the tasks God sets before them.

So we find that age is not always a clear indication of one's capabilities. Likewise, age does not always define who is a man and who is not. I've personally seen teenage boys who act with more maturity and responsibility than some thirty- to forty-year-old men.

David continued his conversation with Saul by telling him some of his past experiences in order to assure him that he was more than capable of carrying out the task before him.

> And David said unto Saul, "Thy servant kept his father's sheep, and there came a lion, and a bear, and took a lamb out of the flock: And I went out after him, and smote him, and delivered it out of his mouth: and when he arose against me, I caught him by his beard, and smote him, and slew him. Thy servant slew both the lion and the bear: and this uncircumcised Philistine shall be as one of them, seeing

he hath defied the armies of the living God." And David said moreover, "The Lord that delivered me out of the paw of the lion, and out of the paw of the bear, he will deliver me out of the hand of this Philistine" (1 Sam. 17:34-37).

David was not simply operating out of zeal; he knew that he was in the will of God. He wasn't just going after this Philistine for sport, but he desired to defeat anyone who dared to come against the armies of God. Plus, David had an undeniable experience with God from his past that gave him even greater faith to know that God would deliver into his hands the Philistine's head. David had a real testimony of God's faithfulness. David knew that the size of the giant in comparison to his boyish frame did not matter. It would not be him fighting in his own might, but it would be the Lord fighting for him, using him only as a vessel.

So what else could Saul say besides, "Go and the Lord be with thee" (1 Sam. 17:37). Saul placed upon David his armor and helmet, but David, in his humility, removed the armor and helmet stating to Saul, "I cannot go with these; for I have not proved them" (1 Sam. 17:39). David had respect for Saul's leadership and skill, even though Saul may have been mocking David by placing the heavy armor on him in the first place.

Part of being a man is the ability to humble one-self under the authority of sound leadership and to respect what that position stands for. Throughout David's servitude, he knew that he would someday take Saul's place and rule as king, but he never lost respect for Saul's authority and position. Instead,

27

The Little Boy in Me

David remained loyal to Saul and continued to serve under him until his appointed time as king. Because of David's obedience, David found favor with God time and time again. He slew the giant and removed his head as promised. In turn, David's faith and victory brought fear on the remaining Philistines and brought about a newfound faith in God amongst the men of Israel.

In 1 Samuel 17:52 we see that after David had slain the giant "the men of Israel and of Judah arose, and shouted, and pursued the Philistines...And the wounded of the Philistines fell down by the way to Shaaraim, even unto Gath, and unto Ekron."

As a man you must learn to lead, not by word of mouth, but by example. "How do I know if I'm a leader?" you might ask. The answer is simple. If you're in a leadership position and no one is following you, you're probably not leading. Part of being a good leader and man includes the ability to first humble oneself under the leadership of a good leader.

After David came under the full leadership of Saul, 1 Samuel 18:5 states that "David went out withersoever Saul sent him, and *behaved himself wisely*: and Saul set him over the men of war, and he was accepted in the sight of all the people, and also in the sight of Saul's servants" (italics added). Notice that David—even after this great victory over the Philistines— did not become arrogant, but the scripture says that David behaved himself. Likewise, we as men need to exercise patience and obedience, listen to leadership, act with patience, and use the wisdom of God concerning life's decisions.

CAST DOWN BUT NOT DESTROYED

Upon realizing the call of God on my life as a young boy, I rushed to my pastor with this information. I always knew I wanted to preach, but now I was ready—or so I thought.

"Pastor," I explained, "I've been called into the ministry and now I'm ready to preach."

"Oh yeah? Well, meet me here at the church tomorrow bright and early," he replied.

Needless to say, the next day I was there long before the intended time. To my dismay, however, I was not met by the pastor with a microphone for preaching, but instead I was met by the pastor's assistant holding a mop and a broom. "You wanna preach? Fine. Start by preaching to these floors," was the message from the pastor. So I obliged. For the next few months I spent my time sweeping, mopping, and buffing the floors of the church. The lesson to me was that I was never going to be anything great until I first learned how to serve.

I'm not implying that this way of servitude is the avenue that men today should choose. Obviously, that is what worked well for me, even though at the time I didn't fully realize how beneficial those moments would prove to be in my future, but God knew. At last, the pastor gave me my "big chance!" It was my turn to preach! I was excited beyond words, and I wanted everyone to come out and hear what I had to say. They did and I preached a message that had everyone on their feet, shouting and dancing all over the place. How did I do such a good job with my first sermon? I preached one of my pastor's messages!

Pleased with myself and not thinking I had done

anything wrong, I approached my pastor in his office after the service. I told him that I wanted to preach more often, to which he replied that I still wasn't ready and pointed out sternly that I wasn't even prepared with a fresh word but instead chose to preach one of his messages.

I was furious at his put down! I ran out of the office, face red and streaked with tears, sobbing uncontrollably. I vowed to never come back. Before I could exit the building, I was suddenly stopped by a hand on my shoulder and someone shouting, "George, what's wrong with you!" It was an older lady, one of the church administrators. I explained to her my plight and how I was tired of the pastor's insults.

"George," she said, "go to the front of the church and count every chair you see sitting up there on that platform." I walked to the front of the huge church and began to count. There were thirty-five chairs on the platform, all for ministers to sit on during Sunday mornings. "Well," she asked, "how many do you see up there?"

"Thirty-five," I answered.

"Yes," she replied, "And what do the persons do who sit there in those chairs?" She paused. "I know Pastor doesn't always communicate very well," she continued, "but he doesn't want you to become like one of those ministers, just sitting in a chair on Sunday mornings, doing absolutely nothing. Sitting on a platform Sunday after Sunday and never having the desire to excel beyond that."

Then it dawned on me; none of the ministers in that church ever did anything except say an occasional prayer and read a scripture on Sunday mornings. They had no ministries outside of that. I knew then that I was going to be different. I would allow God to use me to make a difference in the lives of others. I would not use the title of minister without also accepting the responsibilities accompanying that title. God had used this woman during a very strategic time to place me back on track.

Today I look back on those days and realize that it was the hand of God molding and shaping me into who I am and who I'm still becoming today. There were many times when my pastor angered me, but I never lost respect for him, nor was I disrespectful. Despite our differences and his mistakes, I understood the call of God upon his life and respected him as a man of God and the one chosen at that time to speak into my life. And I honestly believe that one of the reasons today that I gain that same respect from others is because of the law of reaping and sowing. One of the principles I share with my congregation is to *behave yourself today because you don't know who or where you're going to be tomorrow.*

THE JEALOUS BROTHER

Sometimes as men we like to hold titles of great significance, but we lack the knowledge and experience that should accompany those titles. As a result, we not only hurt ourselves but also those around us who are depending on us to get the job done. We resort to cover-up tactics instead of confessing that we're not able to get the job done or that we made a mistake. Maintaining the façade of "superman" becomes more important than growth.

Let's examine the story of Cain and Abel. Here we have two brothers, one who was a shepherd, the other a tiller of the ground. Both went before the Lord to offer up a sacrifice. Cain offered to the Lord the fruit of the ground while Abel offered the "firstlings of his flock and the fat thereof." Abel's offering was received by the Lord, but Cain's was rejected. "And Cain was very wroth, and his countenance fell." So the Lord asked Cain, "Why art thou wroth? And why is thy countenance fallen? If thou doest well, shalt thou not be accepted? And if thou doest not well, sin lieth at the door" (Gen. 4:5-7). God explained to Cain that there was no reason for him to be upset when all he had to do was repent and offer an acceptable sacrifice. Then he could receive the same blessing as his brother Abel. But Cain was stubborn and childish. Jealousy and immaturity clouded his thinking, and, after conversing with his brother in a field, Cain killed Abel.

Now Cain created an even bigger problem. Yet even in the midst of his final opportunity to repent, Cain still chose to do things his way. Little did he know that warring against God is indeed a losing battle; it's God's way or no way at all. God asked Cain, "Where is Abel?" Instead of confessing and repenting, Cain decided to lie and cover up what he had done with sarcasm. "I know not: Am I my brother's keeper?" So the Lord rebuked Cain, "What hast thou done? The voice of thy brother's blood crieth unto me from the ground" (Gen. 4:10).

Because of his disobedience and immaturity Cain was cursed. "And now art thou cursed from the earth, which hath opened her mouth to receive thy brother's blood from thy hand; When thou tillest the ground, it shall not henceforth yield unto thee her strength, a fugitive and a vagabond shalt thou be in the earth" (Gen. 4:11-12). Cain behaved as a child and tried to bellyache his way out of his punishment. "My punishment is greater than I can bear," Cain complained to God (Gen. 4:13). Still, he didn't acknowledge his wrongful act against his brother. It was all about him, what he wanted and the inconvenience that this curse was going to cause him. Cain was now worried about someone taking away his life, never taking into consideration the life he took—his own brother's.

He still did not repent. "Behold, thou hast driven me out this day from the face of the earth; and from thy face shall I be hid; and I shall be a fugitive and a vagabond in the earth; and it shall come to pass, that every one that findeth me shall slay me" (Gen. 4:14). The wonderful thing about God is that in spite of our shortcomings, He is still merciful. In the next verse God displayed His mercy by protecting Cain's life: "Whosoever slayeth Cain, vengeance shall be taken on him sevenfold. And the Lord set a mark upon Cain, lest any finding him should kill him" (v. 15).

LEADING BY EXAMPLE

Many times men who are fathers chastise their children for doing the exact same thing that they are guilty of doing. In the preceding story, we see Cain having a tantrum, making excuses and bad decisions instead of choosing the mature approach. Men today are guilty of this same thing. They tell their children to stop pouting for not getting their way, but these same men scream and fight with the children's mother just because things didn't go their way at work or because they didn't get their way at home.

When I counsel men, I always tell them to lead by

example. In other words, don't tell your child to stop watching so much television when the child sees you up late at night and throughout the day channel surfing. Don't tell the child not to steal when he hears you bragging to others about how much you got back on your income taxes from cheating. Likewise, you can't be a leader in the church, telling others to trust God when you're not a tither. You don't trust God enough to take care of you, so you steal from Him instead.

You can't be a successful supervisor on your job if you're lazy and refuse to make sacrifices, yet you pout when the promotion passes you by. These are all mixed messages. Unfortunately, men who struggle with this little-boy syndrome tend to also birth little boys who never grow up, whether they are natural children or other male figures whom they influence on a daily basis. That's why I try to use extreme caution when appointing men in the church over certain departments. What you say and do as a man has the potential to make or break someone else's life. Men must learn to lead by example, not just by word of mouth.

PROMISES, PROMISES

In counseling many married couples, one of the major complaints I hear from women is that their husbands have big dreams but no initiative, or that they lack integrity as it relates to displaying responsibility and leadership within the family. Promising to change but showing no change is a classic example of a little boy in operation. How many times have you as a man promised your wife that you would be more respectful, or vowed to your children to give them more attention or to take care of their daily necessities, only to find yourself unable or unwilling to follow through on those promises?

When a man begins to really develop into becoming a true man by example and word, he no longer has to make a lot of promises. Instead, people around him begin to simply honor his word with no hesitation. His history gives him past data that his word is his bond. Of course, things do happen in all of our lives to offset some of our greatest intentions, but even when things go wrong, a real man will do his best to right the wrong that has been committed. It's the little boy in us who resorts to cover-ups and pouting like Cain did.

THE VALUE OF TRANSPARENCY

On the surface, Cain seemed to be fine and had no problem with God or Abel until God refused his sacrifice. It was then that Cain's true character really came out. That is why I understand and teach the importance of transparency. Be who you are and never give into the temptation of phoniness. Real men are transparent. Transparency doesn't mean you have to go around revealing to everyone the secret details of your life, but it does mean to be yourself and to work on those areas that need to be strengthened instead of trying to cover them up. If you are honest about your weaknesses, people will not panic if a weakness comes forth in the midst of a crisis. They will know this is an area you are working on, and your ministry and character can remain intact.

Always remember this point: *Who you are in the*

heat of the battle is who you really are. Think about it! Have you ever seen someone in a rage and going off about something that you felt was quite trivial? You may have been shocked or even appalled by their behavior. Well, maybe you never took the time to know the real person, or perhaps they spent so much time being phony and super-spiritual that you were deceived. Whatever the case may be, this is who they really are. And yes, we all have that tendency within us to do things when we're upset that we would not normally do, but when we admit that we have those tendencies to flare up, people are not shocked when they actually see it.

Our honesty allows them to become more receptive of our "other side," and they have a better desire to help us through our trials instead of turning away in disgust. It's when we're phony that we run the risk of losing everything.

So be transparent, and stop trying to be superman and fooling everyone into thinking "you have it all under control." The only person you're really fooling is yourself.

Donald's Testimony

Some men are so egotistical they can't even be honest with God. I'm sure we've heard it many times, "Lord, whatever is in me that is not like You, take it away." The egotistical man says this prayer often. He's super-spiritual, loves the Lord with all his heart and soul (or so he claims), believes himself to be blameless and without sin. *God knows my heart*, this man says to himself. In fact, he may love the Lord with all his heart, but he's also very phony.

He boasts of great victories over the temptations

of Satan and his evil attempts to get him to stray. But he never once shares the real testimony that could actually help someone else—the story of how he *did* stray, but God delivered him out of the situation and covered him at the same time. We see it all too often, this religious spirit that will not allow a man to confess even to God his weakness. Thus, the thing he fears the most comes upon him.

For instance, Donald* knew he had a problem with women; besides, he'd had more than one extramarital affair already. But the church Donald attended taught that once you're saved, "old things are passed away; behold, all things become new" (2 Cor. 5:17). *Glory to God, it's just that simple,* Donald thought. Or is it? This church failed to teach that it takes conscious effort for all things to become new. No one told Donald to be honest concerning his problem, or to let the pastor know so that he would have a spiritual covering, and to be honest with God in prayer so that he could be set free, then to "resist the devil, and he will flee from you" (James 4:7). Instead Donald told no one, not even God, who knows all things, what his problem was. For some time, Donald handled his deception well.

Then "she" came to the church. Her name was Tyler** and upon seeing her, Donald knew he was in trouble. But instead of staying away from her, Donald decided that he was going to "make the devil a liar." Not giving the devil the pleasure of causing him to run from anything became his motivation of denial, and ultimately the trap that Satan used to deceive him, he also used to capture and almost destroy him.

So there she was. The trap was set and Donald

*not his real name
**not her real name

eventually fell. And because this time Satan not only wanted Donald to fall , but also wanted to destroy him, everything about this affair became public knowledge. His wife knew, his children knew, and all of his co-workers and those in his church knew. He was left with no family and because this trial began to affect his ability to work and concentrate, Donald soon lost his job as well. His children resented him and because he'd been so phony, his so-called friends in the church could not understand how he had found himself in this predicament.

A HUMBLING EXPERIENCE

Everywhere he went, it seemed that there were whispers and gossip that raced past his ears. And the other woman—she finally moved on and Donald never heard from her again. He was at his all-time low. What was he to do? Donald had two options. He could either confess, repent to God and his family, and make a change, or he could be like Cain—make excuses, and continue the lying and phoniness—covering up instead of confessing the wrong and making it right. By this time he knew he was at the end of his rope, so Donald chose to repent and allow God to change him from the inside out. Although God forgave him immediately and he was able to salvage his family, it would take Donald years to recapture the trust of those he betrayed and to piece his life back together again.

No longer could he hide behind a religious spirit or his position in the church. By the grace of God, he was who he was, and by the mercy of God, he would find the strength enough to change. He put away his self-righteous way of thinking and instead allowed the Lord to have his way and strengthen those weak areas in his life. Cast your cares upon the Lord because He does care for you (1 Pet. 5:7), and He will see you through each and every weakness that presents itself in your life. But first you must learn to be honest; there is nowhere to hide.

The mature male knows that he must face his failures and weaknesses, not run from them. It's the little boy inside who wants to cover-up issues or crawl into a corner and hide. It's the little boy who keeps you from trusting anyone else, yourself, or even God. The little boy hiding inside wants everything to be done his way, to go his way, and he rebels against submission to his elders and the ones whom God has ordained to lead and direct him in the right direction.

Why is the word *humility* such a harsh word in the ears of men? It's partly because this word has been vastly misunderstood and misinterpreted. Humility is simply the ability to lay aside one's own selfish needs long enough to receive from others. Unfortunately, many men look at the word *humility* as a "dirty word," instead of as an opportunity to better themselves and excel to the next level.

First Peter 5:5-11 gives us a better understanding of the importance of this word—*humility*.

> Likewise, ye younger, *submit your-selves* unto the elder. Yea, all of you *be subject one to another*, and be clothed with *humility*: for *God resisteth the proud, and giveth grace to the humble.*
> *Humble yourselves therefore under the mighty hand of God, that he may exalt you*

> *in due time:* Casting all your care upon
> him; for he careth for you. Be sober, be
> vigilant; because your adversary the devil,
> as a roaring lion, walketh about, seeking
> whom he may devour: whom resist stead-
> fast in the faith, knowing that the same
> afflictions are accomplished in your
> brethren that are in the world. But the God
> of all grace, who hath called us unto his
> eternal glory by Christ Jesus, after that ye
> have suffered a while, make you perfect,
> establish, strengthen, settle you. To him
> be glory and dominion forever and ever.
> Amen (italics added).

So humble yourself and trust in God. In doing so, He will exalt you in due time—in His time. Be wise in your decisions. Don't be hasty and ignorant, making wrong decisions out of your own limited knowledge. Use the wisdom of God and the advice of those He has placed in your life to watch over you. The devil looks for any opportunity available to prey upon your weaknesses, but when you're covered by the blood and by those who care about you, Satan must be forced to use more creative means to get to you.

So don't make it easy for him. Trapping and deceiving you becomes a much harder task when you play on the winning side. We all have different circumstances in life that we must deal with and overcome, but God is the one who molds and shapes us into His perfect image. And to God belongs all the glory, the honor, and the praise for the strength and stability that He blesses us with and the victory we experience over the attacks of the enemy. Yes, you do have the right to change your present circumstance, but it's up to you to take advantage of those rights and put them into action!

Part 2

Lover-
Boy
in Action

The Things We Do for Love

4

He Says She's Just a Friend

Men Who Enjoy the Pleasures of Relationship but Refuse to Commit

While Phillip sat there holding his head in disbelief, trying to figure out just how he'd ended up in this predicament, I sat next to him wondering how he could have missed the obvious. Phillip had been going out with Allison on the weekends for the past two months. "Nothing serious," he constantly reassured himself and others around him. "We're just friends." But because I knew how males and females think differently when dating, I found it a necessity to say something before the so-called friendship turned stale and got out of hand. I decided to speak to Phillip first, so I called him into my office.

I explained to him that under no circumstances do we allow the women in our church to be handled negligently, and that if he were interested in Allison he must go about the relationship with dignity and respect, keeping in mind that her emotions are at stake. And if he had no desire to pursue the relationship earnestly, then he must be honest with her regarding his intentions.

Upon hearing this advice Phillip looked at me dumbfounded and said, "Pastor, what are you talking about? Allison and I are just friends. She knows this and so do I. There's nothing more to it." I knew by this statement that Phillip was not only naïve concerning women, but he was also in trouble. Phillip was in way over his head in this relationship, and he didn't even know it.

So without saying anything further I excused Phillip from my office and called in Allison. After she sat down, I asked her a series of questions. "Allison, how do you feel about Phillip?"

She replied, "I think he's a nice guy. He's really sweet."

So I continued, "Are the two of you just friends, or is he someone you've really grown to care about as something more than just a friend?"

"Well, Pastor," Allison began, "I really like Phillip, and we've been spending a lot of time together lately."

So I concluded with the ultimate question, "Is he someone that you would like to spend even more time with or perhaps even someday marry?"

To which Allison responded, "Sure, why not? I

love the way he treats me and we have a great time together." Needless to say, the conversation I had with Allison confirmed to me what I'd known all along. She was taking this relationship, or so-called friendship, much more seriously than Phillip—her friend.

After relaying to Phillip the seriousness of this relationship, his mouth hit the floor. "How could this have happened, and when did I lead her to believe that things were more serious than they are? Besides, she knows that I'm involved with someone else"—these were all the questions Phillip asked. Now he would have to confront the situation and jeopardize what could have been a great friendship between two individuals.

The Surrogate Mother

Unfortunately, caught in the middle of the immature tactics of men are innocent, and somewhat naïve, women who, despite this man's obvious signs of immaturity, still find him irresistible. This is because the minds of many of these men are so clouded by selfishness that they do whatever it takes to fill the constant voids in their lives. In other words, these men can be very charming if it gets them what they want. But if in the process of meeting their own needs they step on the emotions of the women who pull them near, then so be it.

The truth of the matter is that men should use extreme caution in handling every relationship in their lives, whether it's a business relationship, friendship, or family member, but especially if it's a relationship with women. Too many men today complain of receiving a "bad rap" and damaged reputations, all because they did not handle with care the women who were innocently pulled into their web of insecurity and immaturity.

Because women are natural-born nurturers, an insecure, immature man can be a magnet to her while she's totally unaware that she's even being drawn to this type over and over again. We see it all the time. A woman breaks off one relationship, only to fall for another man who is equally immature— different face, different name, but same person.

How does this happen? Immature men who carry this little-boy syndrome are very dependent on the nurturing and mothering of women. And women, oftentimes, are too eager to give away their love and nurturing. She's the magnet of mothering and nurturing; he's the metal that draws her near with his dependency and boy-like tendencies.

In this chapter let's take a closer examination of these giving women who continue to be used as surrogate mothers to the men who leach onto them refusing to be weaned. As a man, you can be set free from harming the woman in your life who has been playing the mother-game to your needs and learn how to become independent and respected by her instead.

Notice the actions of women who cater to the needs of immature men. They are usually very careful to behave in a very restrictive manner in the man's presence. Usually, she only tolerates him and remains in the relationship because of his ability to be a wonderful love partner to her; plus, she is convinced that without her he will not properly take care of himself. But because he is usually so busy having his needs fulfilled by her giving nature, he never takes into consideration her need for attention from him as well. As a result, she resorts to very creative tactics to capture his attention. Unfortunately, however, these tactics rarely ever work. Unlike her, he is not a very emotional person, so even when she does make subtle attempts to get his attention, he rarely notices.

Even when he does recognize signals for attention, he's oftentimes too insensitive to respond or just "too busy." The unselfish love and attentiveness that she shows to him is not reciprocated simply because he is too preoccupied with meeting his own desires and needs. In tolerating this man she makes herself miserable and conciliates by stroking his back, always making excuses for him, and taking him back. Her unreasonable hope keeps her in this relationship without him even trying to change. She tells herself, *If I can just continue to be strong, things will get better.* She has created an illusion for herself in order to have peace. And when the illusion comes face-to-face with grim reality, she's left with a sour taste in her mouth that suggests *men are just no good!*

ALL MEN ARE DOGS

In order to understand why many women refer to men as "dogs," let's first study the nature and being of a dog. Dogs are domesticated wolves. Thus, in order to track the history of a dog, one must oftentimes consult the history of a wolf. Dogs are carnivorous animals with a vast variety of breeds and genetics. And, in detecting certain smells, dogs have proven to be much keener than mankind, which makes them very useful in hunting.

We know in order to effectively train a dog, it's

best to begin at the puppy stage. If training doesn't start until the dog begins to grow into adulthood, the challenge to break his bad habits—such as wetting on the carpet instead of going outside and chewing on things he shouldn't— becomes an even more tedious task. Dogs may attack viciously when they feel threatened, but, ironically, dogs also make great companions.

Biblically speaking, there is nothing positive about the connotation of a dog. Dogs are used in the Bible to describe anything of low standards or perverse nature. Anyone or anything that is insignificant is often referred to as a dog.

After analyzing the characteristics of a dog, many women would sarcastically agree, "Yes, indeed, all men are dogs." This is because of the stereotypical characteristics that many men have unfortunately paved as a path for all men. When asked to describe men, many women see a wolf in sheep's clothing instead of the loyal companion guarding the door. It's been said that men look upon women as nothing more than meat used to satisfy their huge appetites. And, as it relates to women who are vulnerable and have been hurt, he can pick up her scent a mile away.

Likewise, we should also remember that there is usually one man in every woman's life whom she finds it almost impossible to totally cut off from her life. She daydreams about him even after they've both moved on. The two of them no longer even keep in touch, she doesn't even know where he is or who he's with, but left lingering in the back of her mind and heart is the residue of this man. The impact he has made in her life is so strong that she continues to ask herself, *What if...? What if things had been dif-*

ferent? What could we have done to salvage the rela-
tionship? Where is he now...who is he with . . . is he
happy . . . and if only I could see him just one more
time!
Why is she so vulnerable to this man? Oftentimes
it's because of the so-called investment that she
feels she has placed in this person. *The two of us*
have a history together, she reasons. *Why should*
someone else reap the benefits of my investment? So
she refuses to let him go.

When asked the question, "Why didn't you just
leave this man when he cheated on you?" I've heard
many women explain, "Why should I allow some
other woman who just came into the picture to reap
the benefits of my many years of investment?" This
is not to imply, however, that leaving is always her
best choice. Marriages are filled with challenges,
struggles, good times, and bad times. Every couple
must approach each new challenge with godly
direction, wisdom, and careful consideration of the
mental and emotional repercussions of choosing to
end or attempting to repair the relationship.

Many women believe that in order to have a
"good man," he must be *weaned* at the puppy stage.
In other words, no woman wants a man planted in
another woman's soil. She does not desire the
tedious task of uprooting him, but because, ironically, he is also considered as a great companion,
simply referred to as "just a friend," she decides to
endure.

So, "All men are dogs," becomes the only expression that women can find to say what they really
want to tell men. And that is simply, "Why do men
behave like boys; and how can they hurt without a
conscience?"

51

The Little Boy in Me

In actuality, we all must understand that there is an inherent part in all of our nature that must be disciplined, or tamed, so to speak, in order to maintain good character. As with the proverbial saying, "Curiosity killed the cat, but satisfaction brought him back," many find it thrilling and somehow satisfying to engage in the forbidden, the unmentionable, and take risks even to the point of endangering another person's emotions. This lewd satisfaction of engaging in the forbidden eventually becomes the trap from which this person refuses to break free. So he makes excuses for his behavior. For both men and women, these excuses become a way of escape, drowning out their consciences and godly convictions.

Living with oneself becomes much easier, now that a reason has been created—a *good* reason for *bad* behavior. So knowing that we all have the ability to carry out this type of animalistic behavior, one must ask, "If *all* men are dogs, are women also classified in this or some other more horrendous category? And what about your son, your brother, your father—are they inclusive or the exceptions to the rule?"

Two Different Women Same Attraction

Two types of women tend to fall for the man struggling with the little-boy syndrome. The first is one who gives and gives of herself unselfishly. The problem with this overly charitable woman is that in extending herself so unselfishly, it becomes abusive on the part of the man when he does not reciprocate this giving nature by fulfilling her needs at the same time. She continues to empty herself while he continues to fill up. And because this woman is usually dealing with her own insecurities, his dependency gives her a false strength and distorted hope that "things will eventually get better." Her unrealistic hope convinces her that patience and endurance will cause him to change.

The fact of the matter is, only the hand of God can change him. Sadly, however, many men never even enter into true relationship with God, much less experience the power of His deliverance. Women must realize that it has to be the man's decision and willingness to change. The only thing she can do to help him is to remove her hand long enough for him to become independent and grow up, even if this means sacrificing or losing the relationship altogether.

The second type of woman, however, is more secure with herself and desires personal growth, understanding, and mutual respect in the male/female relationship. Her one weakness, however, is her love for the unexpected. And because immature men usually reign in the area of spontaneity (mainly due to instability), she blocks out the obvious and instead feeds off of his fun character and popularity. But it's when this woman finally sits down to serious conversation with the man that she decides in order for the relationship to work he must grow up. If he refuses, she's finished with him…gone! And although she's not quite sure why things didn't work out, she's also not going to "tough it out" long enough to perform the impossible, which is try to "make" it happen. Men, anytime you are in a relationship with a woman and you hear words like, "We can *make* this work," the relationship is already in serious jeopardy. True

53

relationships are not forced; they're mutually welcomed.

KNOW YOUR LIMITATIONS

It's easy to see why most men fall for woman number one, the mothering type, as opposed to woman number two, whose tolerance for his behavior is at a totally different level. Immature men always need the bosom of a woman to cry on. This type of man preys on her pity and arouses her sympathy to soften her up, even though he knows she's upset with him because of his refusal to grow up. He knows that despite his many tantrums, she will understand and give him another chance. Even when she threatens to leave, he cries with remorse, convincing her that without her, his life is meaningless and that he simply cannot go on.

Some men may resort to worse tactics, such as getting drunk, crying fake tears, and so on. When all else fails, then comes the ultimate drama: screaming, slamming the fists down, slamming doors. He boasts of an authority that he actually lacks and then uses all the wrong tactics to acquire it. Some men even use the game of allowing her to walk out for a short period of time, just long enough for him to be single again and have his "freedom." He knows, or at least he thinks, that when he wants her back, he'll simply "pull her strings." He knows which buttons to push when he wants her back. If this man does not change, then this woman will eventually become fed up and seek the love, affection, and respect she needs from somewhere else—in the arms of another man. Unfortunately, divorce courts are filled with men who refuse to grow up and women who are simply tired of mothering them.

Single men mistakenly feel that they are exempt from the rules and unwritten laws that govern healthy relationships. Dating a woman on a consistent basis and telling others that she is "just a friend" is not a valid safety feature when the friendship/relationship goes sour. As a man and a respectable person altogether, you must be held accountable for your immature actions and the pains they cause to others. One of the first things I say when ministering to single men is this: "You cannot date a woman on a consistent basis and be ignorant of the fact that her emotions are involved." Date her long enough and eventually she is probably going to look at you as more than just a friend. To not take this into consideration is pure negligence and disregard for your female "friend's" emotions. Women are emotionally made up, and it's time that we as men realize that this is something that will probably never change.

If you are a woman reading this book, beware of dating men who keep you a secret. If you have to drive two hours on every date just to go out to eat or to the movies when there are plenty of restaurants and theatres in your area—beware! Why should two single people with mutual interests in each other have to keep such a "tight friendship" a secret? One reason: this gentleman would like to continue seeing you while keeping his options open to other women who are also nothing more than "just friends!"

Women, I've written the next chapter with you in mind particularly. You will learn about the fourteen types of "bad boys," why women find them attractive, and the outcome of those relationships. You'll

The Little Boy in Me

also learn the eight qualities of a good man, plus the key questions you need to ask if a relationship is getting serious. This chapter is a must-read for those who are married or contemplating marriage.

5

Bad Boys

and the Women Who Find Them Irresistible

*A*t a women's conference, where approximately ten thousand women attended, I posed a very thought-provoking question: "How many women are attracted to 'bad boys'?" Without hesitation, more than half the women in attendance at the seminar raised their hands. It's a fact: many women simply find bad boys irresistible and intriguing, but, to their frustration, they are unable to keep them. Why? Because a bad boy, for lack of a better pun, "is just too sexy for his own shirt," and way too sexy not to share his sex appeal with others. For a bad boy, a meaningful relationship is out of the question—not because he refuses to acknowledge one woman as his mate, but because even if he does, she will spend most of her time shooing the flies of other female counterparts who somehow find his sexy, bad boy image irresistible as well. What his mate loves, she can't have; what she holds, she can't keep; and what she tastes, she can't swallow. He is a bad boy, a bad habit that no matter how hard she tries, she simply cannot shake loose.

Many women mistakenly believe that they can change this type of man before marriage, only to find that (in most cases) if he was a bad boy before marriage, he will remain a bad boy after marriage. Now you may ask, "What exactly is a bad boy; what makes him bad; how can I recognize him; or am I a bad boy myself?" Let's investigate the issue further by looking at some of the qualities of the bad-boy syndrome.

Fourteen Examples of Bad Boys

1. **Fresh-Meat Seekers.** This bad boy spends most of his time grooming in order to draw attention to himself. His flirtation ranges from subtle acts of teasing to overt acts of enticement. Although he may not admit it, he constantly needs the approval of others regarding his masculinity and needs a constant companion to stroke his ego. Beware: these boys are easily bored and eager to jump at the chance of pursuing "fresh meat."

2. **Just a Friend.** "I am not ready for a serious relationship" is the warning

heard resounding throughout the life of this man. Though he may even wine and dine the woman in his life, don't be fooled. All the signs are present to her that this man will probably never be ready for the "M" word—*marriage.*

3. **The "Playa" (Player).** Although he may be her tall, dark and handsome knight in shining armor, she may find that a not-so-attractive quality about him is also irresistible—that is, his less-than-gentleman-like behavior. She should not be deceived, however, into thinking that she can change him. This bad boy cannot be tamed.

4. **The Great Pretender.** He assures the lady in his life that together they can move mountains. He assures her that he is the man of her dreams, the one for whom she's been waiting. She should be warned, however, not to get her hopes up too high. He is not the one, but an imposter. He's the great pretender!

5. **The Quiet Storm.** Though quiet in public, this man is an accident simply waiting to happen. One minute she's all he ever thinks about; the next minute he's an explosive combustion of anger. She's not dressed properly; she doesn't look right, walk right, talk right—these are a few of the many excuses he uses for his behavior. In other words, he tells

himself that he is not the problem but his mate is the problem.

6. **Mama's Boy.** This man should read the chapter entitled "Defeating an Enemy Called Self." Indeed, he is his own worst enemy. As long as the woman in his life is there to mother and care for him, all is well in his life. As much as she tries, she simply cannot be this man's salvation. She should not allow herself to be deceived into thinking she can compete with his one true love...his mother.

7. **The Perfectionist.** Ladies, if the man who thinks he's always neater than you gets on your nerves, this is not the man for you. Everything must always be kept in perfect order at all times, and you are no exception to the rule. If you can't abide by his strict rules of order, then this is not the man for you.

8. **The Boxer.** This bad boy never has a need to change because rarely is he in pursuit; instead, he is always the one being pursued. Good looking, but very angry, sexy, yet totally abusive...it's always her fault that her face ran into his fist and bruised her eye. His response is repeatedly, "Look what you made me do," as he helps heal what he knows he's only going to hurt again.

9. **The Gender-Bender.** He appeals to the

feminine side of a certain type of woman. In many cases this woman has come out of the Boxer relationship and has promised herself, "I'll never do that again!" Deeply traumatized through past relationships, she is totally blind to the obvious—he is bisexual.

10. **The Baby-Maker.** Irresistible, sexy, irresponsible, an athlete...he hits a home run every time. His biggest game is playing the fields of females who are in competition with his last, and sometimes present, relationship and who'll stop short of nothing than being able to call him their "baby's daddy."

11. **The Trapper.** Think for a moment, if you are a woman who has tried to leave an abusive relationship many times over a period of several years. Mentally you've left, but physically you just can't bring yourself to doing it. You're probably the victim of "a trapper." Every time you try to leave, he does something or says something to make you stay. As you decide to leave again, it's always over something worse than before. Nevertheless, he knows exactly what buttons to push to change your mind, so you remain ensnared as the seemingly helpless victim of the trapper.

12. **The "Gotcha" Man.** His words are sweet and his appearance sometimes

makes you feel sorry for him. He's the type whose ears are always ready to listen, whose words comfort, and whose embrace is seductive, full of Scripture, sorrowful and repentant. Of course, that's only after he has seduced you into his web of deceit, and now he's sorry. Yet his own selfish desire must be fulfilled—he's a fornicator.

13. **Big Money Grip.** This bad boy is between the ages of 59 to 63, sometimes 70, has a pocketful of money, is usually retired, and loves young girls ages 16 to 32. Although at first the friendship seems very innocent, he is deadly. Her attraction to him is his slender figure, his father-like, almost fading, sex appeal. At a glance, one can tell that he was a stud during his earlier years. His drawing card is cash. From late-night movies to early-morning breakfasts, and the funding of books for school. The lady loves it—until he pulls the string...trapping her in an abusive embrace...it's time to pay up. This relationship always ends tragically. Her rape, his death!

14. **The Promise-Maker-Breaker.** This bad boy is normally in his late forties to early sixties. He possesses many qualities of the aforementioned bad boys. Though retired from his bad-boy image, he has taken on a new, yet equally damaging, position. He is a promise-maker-breaker

and can get anyone to believe that he will come through. In many cases, those who believe that he will come through, he has already disappointed. He preys upon weak women and their children and brings to life the old saying, *A promise is a comfort to a fool!*

'TIL DEATH DO US PART

Of course, we could not discuss the warnings that are embedded in some relationships without also discussing the final stage of becoming one with the right mate—the institution of marriage. Standing at the altar, the bride and groom both make vows, " 'Til death do us part." They make an earnest vow of love and commitment to each other only from that day forward. Caught up in the moment, however, the couple often fails to consider the changes that age and years of growth promise to impose upon the marriage. There's a storm brewing out on the ocean of time that will test the sacred vows of marriage. It threatens to shipwreck marriage and the institution thereof into a place called "no commitment."

Women, especially, should be very cautious when deciding on this very important decision—their permanent mate. Choosing a permanent mate from a temporary location could cause much heartache in the future.

A word of insight to the men: Remember, who she is today is not who she will be next year. A woman is constantly growing, even when her mate may continue to stand still. Her desires, likes, dislikes, and so on will not remain the same because they change along with her continued growth.

The Little Boy in Me

Nonetheless, her growth should not be viewed as a curse but instead as a benefit to the marriage.

EIGHT REASONS MARRIAGES FAIL

Many reasons contribute to the failure of a marriage. Some of these include:

1. Financial instability
2. Distrust
3. Lack of communication
4. Failure to listen or respond
5. Outside influences from friends and family
6. Taking one another for granted
7. Sexual problems
8. Religious differences

Out of these eight reasons, I focus my attention on reason number three—lack of communication. It is from here that much of the problems stem in the life of your marriage. Lack of communication and understanding of one another's deep feelings, emotional needs, financial sufficiency, and physical pleasures strengthens the storm brewing out on the oceans of time, waiting patiently, yet pounding violently upon the shores of marital solitude and joy that each couple is entitled to experience when vowing eternal commitment and love.

Lack of communication leaves the partner to assume and perceive out of his or her own thoughts, which produces a false reality. Whether false or true, to the one who's left to draw his or her own conclusions, the reality of those conclusions becomes as real as facts that are backed by actual data, though no data is present to justify those assumptions. So remember this principle: When communicating with others, what one says is not always what the other party hears. The Scripture teaches, "With all thy getting get understanding" (Prov. 4:6b). Understand one another's likes, dislikes, needs, desires, weaknesses, and strengths. You won't be successful in forcing your mate to change who he or she is, but instead, work together to better those areas that are weak and build on each other's strengths.

Despite marital indifferences, however, one should be careful not to blame problems solely on one individual. Normally, both parties contribute in one way or another to the stress that comes to test the strength of a marriage. Still, the fact remains that in order to maintain a successful marriage, both parties must be willing to adapt to and accept the changes that marriage has to offer.

Knowing and understanding the facets that make up a relationship beforehand better helps in adjusting to change after marriage. During the midweek Bible study lessons at my church, I began to understand that much of our problems stem from simply not understanding the correct meaning of everyday words that we speak continuously but take for granted on a consistent basis. It is said that "a good man is hard to *find*." But I say that unless you're willing to learn about and understand all the facets that make up a successful bond between two individuals, a good man or woman is hard to *keep*. Now let's look a little closer and gain some clarity on some of the words that we often take for granted during the dating process and during times of intimacy with the one we proclaim to love.

The Little Boy in Me

DEFINITIONS[1]

Sex: The property or quality by which organisms are classified according to their reproductive functions. b: Either two divisions, designated male and female, of this classification. 2. The condition or character of being male or female; the physiological, functional, and psychological differences that distinguish the male and the female. 3. The sexual urge or instinct as it manifests itself in behavior. 4. Sexual intercourse.

Sexuality: The condition of being characterized and distinguished by sex. 2. Concern or preoccupation with sex. 3. The quality of possessing sexual character or potency.

Dating: An appointment to meet socially at a particular time; especially with a member of the opposite sex.

Friend: A person who one knows, likes, and trusts. 2. Any associate or acquaintance. Often used as a form of address. 3. A favored companion; a boyfriend or a girlfriend. 4. One with whom one is allied in a struggle or cause; a comrade. 5. One who supports, sympathizes with, or patronizes a group, cause or movement.

Nature: The intrinsic characteristics and qualities of a person or thing. 2. Man's natural state, as distinguished from the state of grace. 3. The aggregate of a person's instincts, penchant's and preferences. 4. The natural or real aspect of a person, place or thing.

QUALITIES OF A GOOD MAN

Certain qualities have been known to make up a good man. Let's expound on a few of those qualities.

1. **Caring.** He is not selfish but is considerate of you and others.

2. **Mature.** He is able to keep his cool in times of adversity, thinks before he speaks, and is very even-tempered.

3. **A Protector.** He understands and cherishes the gift that God gives him in the form of a woman, protects and provides a covering for her.

4. **Honest.** Doesn't make excuses or resort to telling lies to cover up mistakes and failures. He is not afraid to tell the truth and face the consequences in times of adversity.

5. **Stable.** He is not double-minded, changing with the wind on a constant basis. He knows what he wants and is able to make sound decisions, is wise, and financially secure.

6. **Kind.** Treats others as he would like to be treated.

7. **Insightful.** Able to see danger approaching and avoid bad decision-making, as well as lead the family in the right direction.

8. **Communicates Effectively.** Able to communicate clearly and honestly with his mate. Is not withdrawn, refusing to speak or share his feelings concerning pertinent issues.

Do Opposites Attract?

Of course, every good man should be able to enjoy the benefits of having a good woman in his life. Unfortunately, however, this is not always the case. Sometimes a woman is able to bait a man, but because of past relationship traumas, she does not celebrate his good intentions. Though this is not intentional, she subconsciously forces him to pay for what she suffered at the hands of the individual who handled her negligently in the past.

In spite of his caring, unselfish and considerate nature, she doesn't possess these same qualities. She's just out to "get" him—to get everything that she wants. She's inconsiderate, impatient, and doesn't care what others think. And where he's mature and able to keep his cool in times of adversity, she's boisterous, a "cusser," angry, and always talks before she thinks. He's a protector and understands the gift that God has given him in the form of a woman. He protects and provides for her. She interprets his protection of her as control. "Why can't I buy this?" she complains while spending riotously.

He's honest and doesn't tell lies to cover up his mistakes, while she provides no covering in the relationship whatsoever, and all of her friends know of their intimate conversations. His stability is eclipsed by her double-mindedness. She's inconsistent, indecisive, and can't make up her mind—she doesn't know what she wants. She is void of any need to be insightful; besides, he's got that covered. So she remains clueless, blind to the obvious. He's able to communicate clearly and she can't, so she withdraws with statements such as, "Um, hum," "Yeah, whatever," and so on.

It is clear that a relationship of this nature cannot work, yet thousands of relationships survive for several years under these extenuating conditions—it must be the sex! One great philosopher once said that opposites attract. That could be true. The Bible teaches that if you're pleased to remain with the unbeliever, then remain together (1 Cor. 7:13).

A very famous R & B song speaks directly toward the plight of many who've allowed themselves to become entrapped in these unhealthy and unhappy relationships. The artist sings about his displeasure in coming home alone, sleeping alone, eating alone, and loneliness altogether. No matter how bad the relationship is, he just wants someone there with him to fill the void, to cease the silence of his empty abode. These are the sentiments of a lot of people in bad relationships. "I'll endure the abuse and proceed with my plans to marry this person just so I can say I have someone in my life; just so I can have someone to come home to, to wake up to beside me, someone to fill the void of loneliness," only to find that some of the loneliest and unhappiest people of all are those who have chosen someone to fill the void.

Now you may still be asking the question, "Is the 'opposites relationship' a healthy one?" The answer to that is, "sometimes, yes," but "most times, no." Every person must look deep within his or her own blueprint and build upon that. As a pastor, I look deep within my congregation and see many marriages that are absolutely, totally mismatched. Those mismatched relationships have finally been glued together through worship, praise, and a common denominator, which is relationship with God. Their relationship with God enables two individuals (who are committed to dwell with one another) to stay together as long as each of them meets God at a certain time, a certain place each day. God's power to keep people together is evidenced by the individuals who come into the church and often say, "if it weren't for the Lord, there would be no way that the two of us could be together."

Despite what you may have heard, good men do exist. Many times, however, we allow the myths concerning Hollywood relationships to define our outlook of what a good man really is. No, Dexter, from "As the World Turns" soap opera may not exist, but the good man of "The Real World" is alive and well. In the chapters to follow, we will review some of the myths concerning relationships in order to be set free from the pressures of achieving the perfect union, which simply does not exist. If you're thinking about settling down with a potential mate, take the following quiz together first and gain a general idea of how far apart or together your mindset regarding the relationship really is.

How to Spot Potential Problems

1. We can talk about sensitive issues without arguing.
   ___ Yes ___ No

2. He/she helps to build my self-esteem and doesn't tear me down.
   ___ Yes ___ No

3. The amount of affection between my partner and me is sufficient.
   ___ Yes ___ No

4. We both have a sense of humor when together.
   ___ Yes ___ No

5. We don't have large disputes concerning financial matters.
   ___ Yes ___ No

6. My partner has the characteristics of a good parent.
   ___ Yes ___ No

7. My partner has many habits that irritate and disgust me.
   ___ Yes ___ No

8. We would share in making decisions about the household as well as household chores.
   ___ Yes ___ No

The Little Boy in Me

THE POWER OF THE VOW

Remember, there are no perfect people and no quick fixes to relationship issues. Though similarities may exist between couples who are different, each situation is as unique as the individuals involved. Marriage is not easy, but honorable; it's pleasurable, but not always peaceful. In other words, marriage is work. It's the job of both parties involved to make sure that each is doing his or her part to allow it to operate properly. Nobody likes to experience the displeasure of a dysfunctional marriage, so know what you want before you say, "I do," and set realistic goals and expectations.

Something is extremely amazing about the wedding vow. A person can date an individual for several years and never come to the real knowledge and revelation of that person until he or she says "I do." It's almost as if marriage rents the veil (splits it in two) and forces one to see what could not be seen or understood prior to making the wedding vows.

Some people live together outside of wedlock in peace for years, but after they get a marriage license, suddenly it's all over. Couples today voice their fears concerning marriage with statements such as, "It's better for us to stay unmarried because as soon as we get married it's going to cause problems." People understand the challenges that accompany saying, "I do," and I think that the church must not shy away from this issue but face it and address it. People need to understand that the real commitment starts after the vow. The commitment of the relationship seems to be tried much more following the covenant of marriage.

I once interviewed a young lady who admitted

making a mistake by marrying what we defined in this chapter as a bad boy. I asked her, "When did you realize that you'd made a mistake by marrying your husband?"

"The night of the honeymoon," she replied.

To make a lifetime commitment and then have a wake-up call a few hours later only to realize that the union should never have taken place is a devastating way of realizing one's error.

If this is you, don't give up. Although you may have married in haste, God is still capable of turning around what the enemy meant for bad for your good. God's strength is made perfect in your weakness, and His caring arms never fail. Marriage is honorable in the sight of the Lord and should not be taken lightly. With marriages ending in divorce at an alarming rate, you don't have to become a statistic. Invite the Lord into your home and ask Him to show you how to be the best wife or husband that you can possibly be. Proverbs 3:13 says, "Happy is the man that findeth wisdom, and the man that getteth understanding." Ask the Lord to give you understanding, patience, and the wisdom needed to enjoy the benefits of a successful union.

Now that we've examined how the little-boy syndrome plays out in the marriage relationship, we need to shed some light on the other side of the equation—the woman. In the next chapter we will look at the little-girl inside of the woman.

---

1. Definitions are from Webster's Dictionary.

6

The Little Girl in Her

Women, too, have a little girl who never achieved full-grown maturity—the child hidden inside of the woman. However, unlike men who experience the little-boy syndrome, the little girl in women may not be as much of a hindrance to her growth and stability. In fact, my studies have shown that her child-like qualities are not always a curse.

Many things can happen in the life of a young girl to stunt her growth as she enters adulthood. Yet even in cases of traumatizing or stressful situations, the woman possesses within her the resiliency to turn bad situations into positive outcomes by allowing them to work to her advantage instead of her demise. A woman's capability to carry a number of household responsibilities, while at the same time enduring the personal pains, anguish, and distress of her past, is a mystery that only God can fully understand.

In this chapter we will deal with the little girl whose life was interrupted due to issues that only a full-grown woman should have to face. Issues that have both the negative and positive effects on her future. The man in her life must understand and accept both facets of her life (the woman and the little girl), just as she has been willingly to take the time to understand, accept, and sometimes endure his little-boy syndrome as well.

HE UNDERSTANDS I'M AN ORANGE

In my book, *When Loving You Is Wrong, But I Want to Be Right*, chapter 9 is entitled, "Of Apples and Oranges." It is in that chapter, under the heading of "Faulty Relationships," that we distinguish the significant differences between men and women. To explain their differences, we use an apple and an orange. Without repeating the entire metaphor, I will give you the essence of the teaching now.

The apple's skin holds its nutrients and vitamins. The meat of the apple quenches the thirst and satisfies the appetite. The core holds the seeds. In short, the apple is the covering—it is the metaphor for the man.

The orange is pleasant to the eye. The nutrients of an orange are found on the inside, unlike the apple, whose nutrients are mostly found on the outside in its peel. The orange is delicate; if squeezed too tightly it sprays forth its juice upon its aggressor. The best way to get to the meat of the orange and determine the sweetness of its contents is to peel it.

Thus, the best way to get to know the desires, intents, and secret compartments of a woman is to peel her slowly and carefully.

One of the best tools to use in peeling her is constructive conversation. No matter how financially secure, how good looking, and how charming a man is, she will soon become bored with him if he lacks the ability to communicate fluently and openly. It's through his conversation with her that he first becomes intimate with her, as she reveals some of her most secretive truths. And with a good woman, the peeling process involves patience, sincerity, and endurance—qualities possessed only by a good man. Upon peeling her, it's the little boy inside of the man that causes him to instantly ravish, consume, and discard her as yesterday's meal. But it's the full-grown man who understands that even after the orange has been peeled, there's still that thin white layer that continues to cover up what lies behind the most significant part of the orange.

The man, unlike the little boy, understands that a woman is amazing and sometimes very complex. Men, when peeling the woman in your life, use caution. Behind that last layer of skin, be prepared to uncover a number of things from her past that could affect how she responds—or doesn't respond—to you, such as pains inflicted upon her by previous relationships, deep wounds, cuts and bruises, things that her outward layer refuses to reveal. Remember that behind that grown-up and independent person in the form of a woman is perhaps a little girl with issues overlooked, a little girl forced to put away childish things too quickly and assume her role as a woman before her time. So when peeling her, speak to her with kindness and have a caring attitude concerning those things which concern her. Your sincerity and honesty will assure her that you will not handle her with negligent hands as other men did in past relationships, but instead with a gentle and caring heart.

MAMA SAID, DON'T BE PEELED TOO SOON

Sadly, in Christendom many women allow themselves to be peeled and consumed too soon. Normally it's because the girl doesn't adhere to the advice of her mother that she ends up exposed, peeled too soon by a man who didn't take time to handle her gentle structure with care. So there she is—a mess, peeled, with parts of her mental and emotional extremities exposed and dangling in midair.

How many times have we all said, "If only I'd listened to my mother" (or to some other adult who had great impact in our lives)? Now, let's reflect back on some of this much-needed advice and scrutinize some of the areas where many women begin their relationships absolutely wrong. Thus they allow themselves to become prey to a man (or little boy) who lacks the patience to understand that indeed she is wondrously created. She is an orange.

THE THINGS SHE DOES FOR LOVE...DON'T DO IT!

1. **Don't be too aggressive, showing more interest in him than he does in you.** Men become very uncomfortable when women are in hot pursuit, and omit her from even being an option for him as a mate. If he shows her any interest at all, she merely

becomes his pastime when there's nothing else for him to do.

2. **Don't try to buy his friendship or love by showering him with gifts.** This strategy of a woman to capture her "true" love only ends with her being used and eventually discarded.

3. **Don't open up to or fall in love with him too soon.** While I do agree that no woman should open up to a man too soon, I don't believe that she can control when she falls in love with him. A lot of women, believe it or not, are in love with the man even before they open up to the him. Women oftentimes fall in love across the room. They fall in love with the way he dresses, his compassion, personality, physique, and the way he articulates. Most women are irresistibly attracted to a man who can speak and handle himself well. The intimacy confirms what they have already been feeling, so their greatest defense is to stay in control by not revealing too much too soon and not giving themselves so freely. So although they can't control falling in love, they can control the intimacy.

Women must first understand how to take control of their own lives and be content *before* inviting a man into their world of complexities and needs. A woman must also be open to the fact that not every bad relationship in her life was due to the man's immaturity or uncaring nature. Perhaps there are also some little girl issues that she must resolve within herself before trying to meet the needs of someone else.

Timing is everything. While you cannot open up to him too soon, you also cannot expect him to read your mind. Don't get angry with him when he fails to do so and write him off as some insensitive creature in a game of cat and mouse. Remember that he is not the man who ravished you in previous relationships, so don't make him pay for the pains inflicted on you by others.

WOUNDED WOMEN BREED BAD GIRLS

Women who have been hurt in the past and never received the proper counseling and direction tend to manifest their hurt by becoming another character—a bad girl hiding behind the rough exterior of a wounded woman. How many of these women do you know? Or, better yet, have you allowed yourself to become one of these women in your attempt to suppress past pains and go on with life as "usual"?

1. **Holly the Harlot.** Knows what to do to get a man but rarely settles down with just one at any given time. She's the bad boy's best friend, and they both feed off each other's needs. She's the needy little girl giving sex to gain love, while he professes love to gain sex.

2. **Gertrude the Gossiper.** Anything to be liked and anything to gain a friend, and if that includes betraying a friend, then so be it. Though seemingly caring, easily

approachable, and likable, her ability to make you feel comfortable in revealing your most intimate secrets is only part of her scheme to fulfill her cunning plan. Gertrude the Gossiper must gain information and give information.

3. **Bad Mood Margaret.** Something is always getting on Margaret's nerves, but nobody knows what or why. Short temperament, brassiness, and sarcasm are only a few of her qualities.

4. **Tammy the Talebearer.** It's who she is, what she does—born to tell all, reveal all. She's the local newsletter.

5. **Betty the Backstabber.** She professes friendship, but the only real friend she seems to respect is herself. It is said that hurting people hurt other people. Betty is hurt, and her plight in life plays out in the way she treats others.

6. **Heather the Husband Stealer.** If you mess with her, she'll take your man. The institution of marriage has no sanctity to her. For her, the challenge and so-called benefits that she experiences from dating the married man far outweigh the repercussions of these faulty relationships.

7. **Desperately Seeking Sally.** Any man will do. Even the man she says that she'd never look at twice suddenly becomes

attractive. She just wants a relationship for the sake of being able to say, "Yes, I have man." She has not yet realized that she is already complete. The man she seeks will not fill the void of loneliness and insecurity Sally so desperately seeks to fulfill.

8. **Bertha the Butch.** "I have no need of a man," says this woman. Any need that I can't fulfill myself, I'll simply have another woman fill for me.

9. **Religious Rita.** There is no woman virtuous, no not one...except, of course, Rita. Religious, traditional, "spirited," but not spiritual. Unless the man is in her click, no one has enough faith, enough belief, enough integrity—or so she thinks.

10. **Gloria the Gold Digger.** Money talks and that is all Gloria has an ear to hear. Without the cash she doesn't have time to even listen. Good conversation, bad conversation, or no conversation at all, Gloria just wants the cash. This tactic of receiving adequate income has become her sole means of receiving the funds she needs to support her lifestyle.

THE SURVIVAL OF A WOMAN

Although women are natural-born communicators, I think that many of them have had their growth stunted at a very young age, which explains much of their behavior when they become full-grown women. If she is the eldest of her siblings she is many times forced to take on the role of mother, a behavioral pattern which oftentimes spills over into her intimate relationships with men, where she spends most of her time mothering him, neglecting her own needs, totally focusing her attention on making sure that the needs of her "man" are totally fulfilled. If a relationship is to be successful, however, there must be a balance.

Another cause for the stunted growth of women is due to the aggressions brought upon them by men entrusted as caregivers when they were little girls. Whether verbal or physical, no little girl should have to endure the stress of adult sexuality. No matter how mature she may seem on the outside, inside lies a very impressionable mind being molded and shaped by her surroundings. What happens to her as a little girl will affect how she deals with certain issues as a woman, her trust level, compassion, and insecurities. And even if she's not handled negligently by physical means, the words a man says to her as a little girl can also have the same detrimental effects. Remember, she's an orange, and because she's a very young orange, plucking and peeling her could not only endanger her growth, but it could also abort her entire destiny.

Some men use the excuse, "But she's very mature for her age." Regardless of her height or physical stature, she is still incapable of handling the complex emotions that go along with intimacy. When forced intimacy becomes her first encounter with a male/female relationship, it leaves her confused, abused, and unable to make sound decisions as it relates to future intimate encounters. She many times finds herself as a woman going from one male encounter to another—different man, same bad boy. It is my belief that no young girl is able to consent to anything causing such a dramatic change in her life because she does not fully understand the repercussions that this experience will have on her body, mind, emotions, and mental state.

If she is persuaded, however, to engage in sexual activities with a man, she finds herself "searching for love in all the wrong places," making statements like, "He's just a man." She puts every man in the same category as the one who transgressed against her in the past. Her growth is stunted because she became a woman before her time. If the proper counseling and deliverance does not take place, she becomes open prey to the one she categorizes as "just another man."

So when the opportunity does present itself to settle down with a good man who understands that indeed she is an orange, she merely blows him off as "too good to be true." She convinces herself that he's just trying to trap her and puts up her guard. But though she thinks she is protecting herself from this new man, she is really reacting to the man from the past who was entrusted to take care of her as a little girl but betrayed her trust, robbed her innocence, and endangered her destiny. Consequently, she rejects the love she so desperately seeks and desires because of fear that she will only be disappointed again. The reoccurring pains that she hates the most continue to endure. As a woman before her time, the little girl inside refuses to allow her to enjoy the pleasures of a pure and mature relationship between adults.

The miraculous part of this whole scenario is the woman's ability to have all of this hidden pain residing on the inside and yet appear to have it altogether on the outside. This is where we begin talking about her many compartments: sister, daughter, wife, mother, and businesswoman—all disguising the little girl whose growth was interrupted. Just as there are many compartments to an orange, a woman likewise has various compartments.

For instance, she knows that in spite of her marital problems that the stability of the children must remain firm. She knows that regardless of the discipline problems of her children, the marriage must remain on a solid foundation. She knows that in spite of past hurts, pains, and sufferings that she had to deal with as a little girl, she must possess the tenacity and strength to survive as a woman. And that is why it is so important that when she decides to settle down with a mate, he is one who understands that behind her fine layer are imperfections and flaws that only a real man can truly understand. He must understand that there is more to her than the sophisticated stature and beauty that he found irresistible upon meeting her for the first time. *There's more to her than meets the eye.*

SHE'S SO FINE

The power of a first impression! It is here where one is able to distinguish with careful observation the mental, emotional, and psychological differences between the sexes. Because men are stimulated primarily by the physical aesthetics of a woman, their thoughts on the makeup of an ideal woman are no large mystery. Because a man's expectations are normally so unreachable and unrealistic, he sometimes allows himself to venture on an endless journey searching for the "fantasy woman" who simply does not exist. A clear sign of a man trying to fill the void of inadequacy in his manhood is one who often seeks unrealistic feminine images and fantasy relationships. Being overly preoccupied with these superficial mental images of an ideal woman reveals his personal insecurities, lack of self-esteem, and, in some cases, even his arrogance.

This man wants the woman's appearance to be as close to perfection as possible. After all, when she is on his arm, she must be a representation to his peers of his good taste and power to attract such an awesome and phenomenal "catch." Anything less than these standards is certainly unacceptable. For these types of men, no one is good enough, not even his "fantasy woman," for soon he will bore of her as well and discover some flaw to justify his disinterest and readiness to move on.

Strangely enough, however, the same qualities he demands of her are not always reciprocated by his own appearance. While she must maintain the appearance of a princess, he is often afforded the opportunity of sporting a less-than-nobleman-like appearance. What he demands of her, he is unable to return, yet he remains adamant concerning his needs, his wants, his desires.

I once confronted a brother in my church regarding his unhealthy affections toward a number of the women in the church. Upon confronting this young man, many things surfaced out of the conversation, which revealed not only this young man's insecurities and fears, but also his lack of respect toward women. Not wanting to be held accountable for his boyish actions, he blurted out that he didn't allow himself to become too "caught up" with women, but he always maintained control. He said that he chose with *whom* to fall in love, as well as *when* to fall in love. Not only that, but the young lady of his choice also had to meet up to a number of standards set on his list of expectations.

Upon hearing this comment, my wife and I both stared at him in amazement, not believing the words that were coming out of this young man's mouth. "How can you demand so much when you bring so little to the table yourself?" I asked him.

This young man had an unhealthy and ungodly mentality. This type of man has a perverse way of viewing women, which is the result of a stronghold that was allowed to develop but must be cast down. His arrogance and fantasy expectations create his womanizing attitude. Consequently, he is not above mentally or physically abusing women. His motives for securing them in a relationship with himself are selfish and shallow—a mirror of his insecurities. And when he doesn't end up being an abuser, he is usually a romantic failure of some sort, whose self-perception is boosted only when a beautiful counterpart in the form of a woman accompanies him.

Make no mistake: these types of men are not seeking the woman for inward beauty, maturity, or her caring nature. If she does not have the statuesque figure, the radiant glow, and the elegant poise to accent her breath-taking beauty, she is not to even be considered as an option. Overall, these men ask for things they themselves cannot deliver. When unable to find satisfaction, they become content with the distorted fantasy images in their minds, saving themselves for relationships that are figments of their imaginations and that will probably never become a reality. As a result, they settle for simply staying in love with the one they love the most—themselves.

Don't Buy the Lie

Misconceptions concerning true love and the "perfect" mate have been widely accepted. So when both parties allow the love to die in a relationship, it's dismissed as a normal development in a relationship, when often the cause could be more deep-rooted issues and areas of debate. However, one should not always assume that the marriage is in trouble in cases where the intimacy dies down or is not as prevalent as in the beginning of the marriage. Get rid of the myths and take time to know your mate before you marry, and take time to get to know him or her again after you marry. As with any relationship, time brings about change, and change is not always a pleasant adjustment.

Common Misconceptions

1. **Marriage will complete me and give me the joy and happiness I've been missing.** If you're thinking of using marriage to purchase your first-class ticket to happiness, I suggest you think again. If you're miserable with life while you're single, you'll be even more miserable after marriage. Not only that, but you will invite your spouse as the unwilling victim into your misery.

2. **Being married means having plenty of sex, and if my mate doesn't want sex often, then he or she must be having an affair.** You must remember that there are many other factors involved, other than having an affair, when it comes to the lack of sex in a relationship. Although not voiced, one partner may be under a significant amount of stress, which could be the root cause of the problem. Fatigue and bad health could be other contributors. The only way to really determine the cause of the problem is with open communication on behalf of both parties. Women especially should not jump to conclusions, blaming themselves for the lack of intimacy in a marriage. Don't assume anything. Instead, ask!

3. **Open communication means telling my husband or wife *everything*.** Although honesty and communication in a relationship are very important, I suggest you approach with caution those things you feel so compelled to disclose. One should also remember that timing is very important. Telling your spouse something at the wrong time, for instance, when tensions are already high, could have irreversible effects. The best way to avoid lying to your spouse or withholding information is not to do things that you are unwilling or unable to disclose.

4. **My husband or wife should be able to read my mind.** Again, women especially, don't expect your husband to read your mind. Though it is true that after being around each other for awhile, spouses are able to determine each other's mood swings or levels of content and discontent, still one should not assume. Say what you mean, and mean what you say.

5. **It's impossible for anyone to have a good marriage who had a terrible childhood or whose parents experienced a terrible marriage.** I am a living testament that this is not true. Applying the principles of patience, getting rid of the little-girl and little-boy syndromes that cause stress on a marriage, and seeking the Lord's guidance were major contributors to the success of my marriage today.

If you're the type of woman who does not like to talk but instead you give orders, nag, and constantly behave irrationally, then a self-examination is definitely in order. Ask yourself:

1. Am I constantly allowing small things to make me lose my temper?
2. Are my requests irrational?
3. Do I feel in control when I nag and make demands?
4. Do I speak to my husband as my child instead of my grownup husband?

5. Do I find myself belittling him more than encouraging him?
6. Do I complain to my friends and family about the marriage?

If you answered *yes* to at least one of the preceding questions, then your marriage could be gasping for air, barely holding onto its survival. Perhaps it's the little girl inside, the one who refuses to confront the real issues, that causes this irrational behavior. Take time to sit down, talk to your spouse rationally, and take responsibility for your own actions. Sometimes the hardest part of growing up is telling the little girl on the inside that she can no longer have her way, but the woman must now take control.

If you have determined that you are in a marriage or relationship that is on the rocks, you probably wonder what you can do. In the next chapter we'll look at what happens when "judgement day" comes, and we'll also see what God teaches us about judging through the surprising story of Tamar, a woman twice married who had to confront her father-in-law's deceit.

Part 3

The Birth of a Man

It's Time to Grow Up Now

7

Judgement Day

*T*he marriage was over, and on the day of the divorce proceedings his thoughts and her thoughts both took a walk down memory lane. The courtship, the wedding, the marriage, the children, and now the divorce, respectively. What went wrong with this seemingly perfect marriage? Could either one of them have done anything differently to salvage the marriage? And exactly whose fault was it anyway?

He thinks, *If only she'd not been so vocal about everything, such a nag, and so unforgiving.*

While she says to herself, *Why couldn't he just be a man, grow up and take care of me and the family, as he should have?*

The Little Boy in Me

They both willingly participate in the blame game, one passing the blame to the other. As they experience for a moment what seems to be a brief "out-of-body" experience, their minds launch them back to the day it all began. Ironically, however, these varying thoughts end as they both exit the courtroom — now two single individuals. His are thoughts of relief. Although he knows he'll miss the relationship from time to time, still he now feels "free."

Her thoughts, on the other hand, are plans for the future as she instantly feels herself taking on a metamorphosis. One era has ended, and now a new one is beginning. *I can't believe it's finally over*, she thinks, and then she prays, "God, grant me the courage to accept the things I cannot change, and the wisdom to deal with life as a single mother!"

Many women ask the question, *Why are men so final, so harsh, so cold and unaffected by things? Do they even care at all, or is it all just a front in order to maintain that stern, male ego?* Of course, no one can sum up the thoughts, feelings, and emotions of all men, but one thing that may help to bring a little clarity to the situation is for women to understand that men and women are in fact two totally different creatures. So instead of having a battle of the sexes, it is easier for both to simply agree that each is unique, yet wonderfully made, by God.

As it relates to the mind of God, the Scriptures say, "For as the heavens are higher than the earth, so are my ways higher than your ways, and my thoughts than your thoughts" (Isa. 55:9). God made humanity in His own image, but who can question or answer why He made each sex so unique? A woman's security normally consists of stability: she feels comfort in being at one with God, her husband, her family, and friends. If single, her comfort stems from being secure in who she is—self-sufficiency—and in developing a relationship with God.

Men, on the contrary, most often find security in freedom and independence from commitment. A man guards his space with the utmost care, and even in his relationships he may strike out at anyone who crosses the line—his line of independence and freedom. This type of man makes the rules, and if the woman in his life intends to keep him, she'd better learn the do's and don'ts quickly. Otherwise, her suggestion to him for dinner together on Monday night could be construed as overbearing and controlling. *Besides,* he thinks to himself, *she should know better than to suggest such a thing on during Monday night football.* He doesn't consider the fact that she is not a sports fan and has no idea that Monday night in front of the television is his sacred cow.

Which bring us to our next point. It is better for a man to simply tell the woman his true feelings and expectations, rather than assume she has been watching and studying him carefully so that she could learn his log of do's and don'ts. And what about the expectations that he has concerning her— the type of character, personality, tolerance level, and so on she should have? One of the responsibilities of a male in the area of adult development is to boldly voice with clarity his expectations at a level of honor and integrity. But he must also be realistic when establishing these expectations. In other words, "Do unto others as you would have them do unto you."

Don't give people unrealistic expectations that

you know are impossible to fulfill. Holding others to a standard higher than what they are able to meet is a self-righteous attitude that ultimately backfires as one's own sins and weaknesses are exposed. The Bible never tells us not to judge or have certain expectations of others; but it does warn that the same measure we use to judge others will be used to measure us as well (Luke 6:37-38).

GUILTY AS SIN

In the story of Tamar in Genesis 38, Tamar first married the oldest son of a man named Judah, but the Lord slew her husband because of his wickedness. As was the custom, Tamar was given Judah's second oldest son as husband, and he died the same way. When his sons died, Judah never investigated the possibility of sin in his own household. Instead he pointed his finger at Tamar. "Then Judah said to Tamar his daughter-in-law, 'Remain a widow in your father's house till my son Shelah is grown.' For he said, 'Lest he also die like his brothers.' And Tamar went and dwelt in her father's house" (Gen. 38:11, NKJV).

As time went on, Judah's son Shelah became of age, but Judah still did not present him to Tamar for marriage. Instead, Tamar remained a widow, on her own without any means of support except that which came from her father's house. Much of this scenario continues to play out today. Men who make no preparations for the future of their wife and family force these women to return home to father and/or mother's house when difficult times arise.

Notice that in verse 11, Judah tells Tamar to remain a widow, not in *his* house, nor *his son's* house, but in her father's house. So not only does he show a lack of compassion, he also tricks her into an indefinite state of widowhood. Judah, like his sons, leaves Tamar no inheritance. The old saying "drastic times call for drastic measures" becomes a part of Tamar's reality. Tamar learns that Shelah has reached adulthood without her being given to him as his wife (Gen. 38:14b). Because she is left on her own and realizes that Judah has deceived her, Tamar resorts to manipulation and trickery in order to secure her future. Notice that nowhere in the aforementioned text has anything been said about Tamar being a manipulative person. It's only after she becomes one with a family who has this bad seed running through their genealogical order that Tamar finds herself doing things that she might not otherwise even conceive of doing.

In chapter 5 of my book entitled *Oppressionless*, we deal with STD'S—Sexually Transmitted Deceptions and Spirits. Be careful with whom you lie down. The spirit of that person becomes one with you. One need only to be wise of the devices of Satan. The transfer of spirits is alive and real even today.

Because of her frustration and the generational curse that had been transferred to her, Tamar dresses like a harlot and deceives her father-in-law into lying with her. Tamar was so out of character that her father-in-law did not recognize her. "And she put her widow's garments off from her, and covered her with a veil, and wrapped herself, and sat in an open place, which is by the way to Timnath…When Judah saw her, he thought her to be a harlot; because she had covered her face" (Gen. 38:14–15). As the story goes, Tamar lies with Judah and he promises to leave his signet, bracelets, and staff with her until he can send payment. Unbeknownst to Judah, Tamar conceives from their union. Later, Judah sends his friend back to town to give the "harlot" a baby goat as payment for services rendered. To his dismay, however, he finds no harlot, and no one who can recall ever seeing a harlot in that area on the day that Judah laid with her. This makes Judah very nervous, so rather than look for her any further, he backs off, allowing her to keep in her possession the signet, bracelets, and staff. "And Judah said, Let her take it to her, lest we be shamed: behold, I sent this kid, and thou hast not found her" (Gen. 38:23).

Judah probably began to wonder who this woman really was since no one had any recollection of her. He became worried that his hidden deeds would become exposed, thus limiting his ability to be judgmental of others. In Matthew 7:1-5 Jesus clearly gives His point of view about judging others:

> Judge not, that ye be not judged. For with what judgement ye judge, ye shall be judged: and with what measure ye mete, it shall be measured to you again. And why beholdest thou the mote that is in thy brother's eye, but considerest not the beam that is in thine own eye? Or how wilt thou say to thy brother, Let me pull out the mote out of thine eye; and, behold, a beam is in thine own eye? Thou hypocrite, first cast out the beam out of thine own eye; and then shalt thou see clearly to cast out the mote out of thy brother's eye.

Jesus is not commanding us to refrain from judging, but rather to be mindful that however we judge others we should be prepared to be judged the same way ourselves. And if it turns out that our slate is clean, fine. Otherwise, we're what Jesus refers to as a hypocrite—*a person who puts on a false appearance of virtue or spirituality.* The Greek rendering of this word is *hypokrites* or actor. Judging others unjustly turns you into an actor because you have to lie to everyone around you about who you really are. You act out one part, but the real you is kept hidden until you are exposed. Fortunately, your unjust judgement of others becomes the catalyst for bringing about this expedient exposure.

Three months after lying with the "harlot," Judah is told that Tamar "is with child by whoredom. And Judah said, 'Bring her forth, and let her be burnt' " (Gen. 38:24). Here we see a man with self-righteous syndrome—he will cover his own faults but has no mercy when the similar faults of others are exposed.

Because of his lack of compassion, Judah was exposed. "When she was brought forth, she sent to her father-in-law, saying, 'By the man whose these are, am I with child: and she said, Discern, I pray thee, whose are these, the signet, and bracelets, and staff' " (v. 25).

Judah is "busted." What more could he say but acknowledge that indeed he had judged Tamar unjustly. "And Judah acknowledged them, and said, 'She hath been more righteous than I; because that I gave her not to Shelah my son,' And he knew her again no more" (v. 26).

In this case Tamar was blessed enough to have her life spared by having the "goods" on Judah. But in many instances, others are not as fortunate. They

The Little Boy in Me

become lambs led to the slaughter in the hands of individuals who are as guilty or guiltier than they are.

THE MORE MATURE APPROACH

I believe that because of everything that I've gone through in the past, I have an innate ability within me to forgive those whom others would not find worthy of being forgiven. I'm able to forgive easier than most, but I also understand that our battles are not to be taken personally. We're in a spiritual battle. I understand that even with the most difficult individuals, God gave us instructions on how to deal with each person at each level. No two persons are the same.

We find this true even when disciplining our children. As parents we love to say, "I treat all of my children the same." But is this statement really true? Each child in the home is to be dealt with according to his or her character and maturity level. A child, for instance, who is very quiet and withdrawn does not always require the harsh discipline needed for one who is more stern, stubborn, or outspoken in character. Trying to inflict the same punishment on each child can oftentimes cause irreparable damage. Likewise, our heavenly Father knows how much we can bear. He deals with each of us at our own individual levels; thus, he expects us to do the same with others.

In this chapter we've seen how being judgmental will destroy relationships. If you want to preserve a relationship, then the next chapter is essential for you to read because it tells how to create and condition that most relationships never achieve—closeness.

8

Destroying the Barriers

*O*ne of the elements missing in most relationships is the element of closeness. Closeness normally
takes a back seat to the pursuit of other issues such
as love, paying bills, and so forth. In reality, it is
impossible to pay bills, have an outlet for intimacy,
raise the children, plan vacations, and meet each
other's needs without closeness. It's the closeness
that allows two individuals to come together and
structure the daily, monthly, and weekly activities
that make it possible for the sexual need to be met,
the financial need to be met, needs for recreation, as
well as the other vital compartments that make up
the existence of a successful union. All of this
brings me to the next point—communication.

The Little Boy in Me

If there's no closeness, there's probably no communication, and communication doesn't mean just talking. It means the intercourse of words, the intersection of life, proper communication to the other individual that their point was clearly understood. Many times the argument regarding communication is, "You're not listening to me; you didn't hear what I said." One of the real gifts of communicating properly is the ability to effectively relay to one's partner the following messages: *I clearly understand what you are saying to me; we understand each other.* This strengthens the closeness, and closeness forces communication. Communication gives closeness its strength. It's out of the closeness that your relationship flourishes. It's out of the communication that your relationship is going to have meaning.

Finally, without closeness and without communication there will be no conflict, and without conflict there will be no resolution. So our third issue is conflict-resolution. How do we discuss and resolve issues effectively without trying to win the argument while at the same time meeting the need of the other individual?

I'm reminded of a relationship that went on between two individuals who were opposites but had one common denominator—they appreciated and had great regard and respect for one another. They had children between the two of them, and great conflicts would arise concerning family and marital issues. Because there was no closeness and because communication was absolutely lost, there was never any resolution to their conversations.

If your relationship is going to be successful, you must figure out a way to bring a resolution to every conflict. Many times, the task of bringing a resolution to the conflict is very simple. It simply means that both individuals must cease from engaging in the actions that sparked the conflict in the first place. Stop doing what has been found to bring unnecessary conflict between the relationship.

You can be extremely in love with a person and not like a lot of things about them. This is true in many relationships. The sex is great, and from time to time the cuddling is wonderful—popcorn, television shows in the nighttime, early morning talks—these are all nice. Yet at the same time there are a number of things that a spouse may not like or appreciate about the other spouse. These things may cause so much pain that separation and sometimes divorce will occur. Some things are trivial, such as popping gum, or staring off while the a conversation is going on, leaving the cap off the toothpaste, leaving the toilet seat up. Other times it's about finances—spending cash and understanding of how the money was spent. All of those things can produce the type of stress that makes the other individual feel like pulling his or her hair out.

And even when the perceived problem is communicated properly by the person who is offended, the offender many times still does not understand "what's the big deal." This lack of understanding and anger can lead to name-calling and threats of ending the relationship in order to get the other party's attention—in order to shock him into the realization of the severity of the matter. It can also provoke finger pointing, with each party exempting himself or herself from the root cause of the problem, shifting the blame to the other individual. And without one party exhibiting enough bravery to ask for forgiveness and the other party being unselfish enough to forgive, the relationship, or lack thereof, will simply not last for much longer.

Forgiveness is an essential part of any marriage, and it is literally impossible for any relationship to exist without forgiveness. I often say that the true test of forgiveness is allowing the person who offended you to get close enough to you in order to trespass against you again. This idea of forgiveness will take you calling on a Higher Power (the Lord Jesus Christ) in order for this to work in your life. I must also add that I don't think a relationship should revolve solely around you having to constantly forgive an individual for doing the same thing repeatedly. Such a relationship is an abusive one, which lacks the proper elements of conflict resolution previously mentioned.

EFFECTIVE COMMUNICATION VS. SURFACE COMMUNICATION

Now you might say to yourself, "My spouse and I talk all the time. Lack of communication is definitely not our problem." But think about it for a moment. What do you really talk about—paying the bills, what's for dinner, the children? Are you merely discarding the other real issues that make up a family, marriage, and your personal well-being, simply scratching the surface in order to feel good about having seemingly open communication?

What about discussions regarding your desires, dreams, and aspirations for the future? If you or spouse constantly watches television while the other is conversing, then you've probably been living nothing more than a façade. And if both of you sit down and really take time to discuss serious, thought-provoking issues you may find things that have been lying dormant in each other's hearts for years.

Let us now clarify what effective communication entails. Effective communication is the ability to relay one's thoughts, ideas, and concerns regarding pertinent issues to another. Effective communication fulfills a purpose. It brings closure and understanding to many of life's concerns. Communication is not just casually mentioning one's day-to-day routine or saying "hi" in the mornings and "good-bye" at night.

Couples sometimes mistakenly feel that avoiding certain issues is better than confronting them and risking conflict. On the contrary, however, avoiding the issues only prolongs and delays the inevitable conflicts lying dormant, just waiting for the perfect time to surface...usually at the wrong time. When negative feelings, anger, and unresolved issues are suppressed and not expressed, it's a known fact that something will happen to force the individual to confront the situation from which they've been shying away. And because emotions have been suppressed for such a long time, the confrontation in many instances turns toxic and nasty. An anger comes forth that shocks family and friends. It appears that the individual is acting out of character when, in fact, their volcano is just erupting stored debris, a hidden inferno that's just been waiting to inflict its irreparable damage.

HEALING TAKES TIME

Don't be deceived. There is no magic wand to wave and heal the years of damage inflicted on a relationship that has lived its life in a façade, a fantasy world of existence. There are, however, proper steps one can take in order to correct those things which were done in ignorance and perhaps salvage what can be a wonderful union. Before actually sitting down to talk, both parties must decide that they are willing to be open and honest, otherwise, the contractual agreement to communicate has already been breached. Let's first begin with the following steps and go from there:

1. **Tell your partner how you really feel without pointing the finger.** This is not the time to point a finger at the other party or shift the blame, but to get results. During this stage you must be willing not only to tell how you really feel, but also to receive objectively what the other party is saying, whether good or bad. Without true expression it is impossible to get true results.

2. **Boldly ask for what you want.** Don't use this time to take a jab at your mate, but instead ask for what you want and express your needs in a positive and mature manner. Be prepared to tell why you need what you've expressed as well. I need it "just because" is not an acceptable answer when developing open communication.

3. **Exercise the patience of listening.** Here is where many of us "drop the ball." Talking when we should be listening

causes us to miss many pertinent issues and concerns of the other party. Unimportance of an issue to you does not change the importance of the issue for the other person. Therefore, you should at least afford the individual enough respect to listen to what the problem really is. I often tell the ministers in my church that what a person is complaining about on the surface is normally not what the problem is at all. In order to find out the root cause of the problem, one must exercise the gift and patience of being a good listener.

4. **Don't assume anything.** Don't assume that the other party knows what's bothering you, regardless of how long either of you have been together. For instance, it's proven that what bothers women is, in many cases, of little or no concern to men (and vice-versa). Neither should you assume that you know all the answers. If there is a question about anything, always ask, and be prepared to receive the answer, even if the answer is not a popular one to receive. This is not the time to barge off into a temper tantrum because of information being received that is not pleasant to the ears. Remember, your chance to respond will come when it's your time to speak. If you don't know, ask; if you think you know, ask; if you know you know, *ask!* Don't assume anything, and don't be

intimidated by the potential answers that
you could receive by asking.

This brief list of do's and don'ts is not to imply
that arguments will not erupt or that arguments are
unhealthy. But simply to stress the importance of
confronting the many issues in a relationship instead
of becoming angry and shutting down all lines of
communication. As a matter of fact, it's during
"constructive" arguments that much of the growth
process of relationship takes place, and truth is
really revealed. Don't try to force your partner to
change into someone that he or she is not, and don't
allow the differences in personality and ideas to
intimidate you. Instead, embrace and build on each
person's unique qualities. Look at them as an asset
to the relationship and not a hindrance. Likewise,
don't always wait for the other party to initiate the
conversation. Someone has to be the catalyst for
opening up the lines of communication, and that
person might as well be you!

And remember, mutual respect is not an option,
but a must. You don't have to agree on everything,
but you do have to possess a willingness to hear the
other party's side of the argument without disre-
garding its importance. Women, find out what
moves your husband, what his passions, likes and
dislikes are, and show enough interest to talk to him
concerning those things.

Men, in addition to knowing your wife's likes,
dislikes, and concerns, be patient enough to sit with
her and converse in intelligently about what moves
her. Women are unequivocally moved by and
attracted to men who possess the ability to hold
intelligent conversations and are not selfish but

show enough patience to listen to what her dreams and aspirations are as well.

Now that we have discussed communication and conflict resolution in this chapter, we can move on to a topic that is sure to test those skills—money. In the next chapter, find out how men's attitudes toward money are developed and learn the spiritual principles of financial freedom.

9

M & M

Men & Money

*By much slothfulness the building
decayeth; and through idleness of the
hands the house droppeth through. A feast
is made for laughter, and wine maketh
merry: but money answereth all things
(Eccl. 10:18).*

Man was placed in the life of woman to
protect and care for her and to be the stability and
caretaker of the family. Of course, today much has
changed in a world where we have male home-
makers, single-parent fatherhood, and stay-at-home-
dads. But these modern domestic situations still do
not negate the fact that men must have some form of

financial stability and set an example to the generations looking up to them. Slothfulness and complacency have been the major hindrances between the man and his success.

Before we go over specific guidelines on how to manage your finances, we must understand that success is not defined as solely having cash in the bank. Many of the traditional prosperity messages have failed due to bad teaching and greed—*get all you can, and can all you get.* It has become a case of bargaining and gambling with God to acquire the things we want—giving money to get money. The church is not supposed to become a religious stock market and Sunday Morning casino. While I do believe in sowing into the kingdom of God and expecting an increase, I do not believe in always sowing exclusively to get something in return.

Though it is the will of God for his children to be prosperous and have their needs met, it is not His will that we use Him as a slot machine. Instead we're to be responsible men with godly intentions, able to be trusted with hundreds before He releases to us thousands, or perhaps even millions.

GAMBLING IN THE HOUSE OF GOD

You don't have to bargain with God to move Him on your behalf. Obedience to God is better than sacrifice (1 Sam. 15:22). When we obey what His Word says, we no longer have to end up sacrificing by giving to God what rightfully belonged to Him in the first place. Everything we need has already been prepared and made available to us through His Son Jesus, even before the foundation of the world. It's the enemy, Lucifer, who blinds our thinking and understanding of the Word of God so that we miss out on the blessings that God has already prepared and ordained for us to have.

You will never be successful until you first realize that, as an inheritance, Jesus left to us the rights of success. You have to recognize that God has already created within you the means of maintaining a successful and prosperous life on earth. Regardless of how much money you obtain, you can still fall into the trap of living an impoverished life unless you learn how to make your money work for you instead of you working for your money.

I'm sure we've all heard horror stories of people who "hit it big" winning the lottery and obtaining millions, only to find themselves once again in financial ruin and broke within a short period of time. This is because you must first have the mind of a millionaire before you can successfully handle being a millionaire. Being a millionaire is not just cash. You need to ask God to first make you a millionaire in favor. This means that even if hard times come, the favor of God will still open doors for you to obtain the things you need in order to maintain a successful lifestyle without having to resort to deceitful and desperate tactics.

You don't become successful the day you have a million dollars. You become successful the day you recognize your potential and begin to put into action God-given directions on how to maintain success at your own individual level. Avoid being driven by the success of others and instead ask God to give you something that you can understand for your life that meets your need.

Living from one paycheck to the next was never the way God intended for man to live. When the

subject of money comes up, most Christians immediately put up their guards—especially men. Even
in the church, when the offering receptacle is
passed, women tend to out-give men every time.
Money has been somewhat of a *dirty word* to men in
the church because of three specific reasons:

- Male ego and pride won't allow men to
  give.
- Self-indulgence becomes more important
  than supporting the ministry God has
  placed over many men.
- Ignorance concerning the Word of God
  causes men to fear when it comes to giving.

When the word *offering* is mentioned from the
pulpit, men don't think to themselves, "Oh, praise
the Lord! It's time to give to God!" No, instead
many say to themselves, "Time to pay the pastor's
salary." It's their ignorance that will not allow them
to give, and it's Satan who seizes the opportunity to
rob them of their blessings. So the man robs God,
and Satan robs the man.

Malachi 3:8 states it clearly: "Will a man rob
God? Yet ye have robbed me. But ye say, Wherein
have we robbed thee? In tithes and offerings." And
because of this robbery, "Ye are cursed with a curse:
for ye have robbed me, even this whole nation."
Now I ask, is stinginess really worth the price one
must pay for holding onto the cash with a tight fist?

This is not a prosperity message, nor is it a "get-
rich-quick-scheme," but giving is a command from
God. "Give, and it shall be given unto you; good
measure, pressed down, and shaken together, and
running over, shall men give into your bosom. For

with the same measure that ye mete withal it shall be measured to you again" (Luke 6:38).

THE POWER OF GIVING YOU REAP WHAT YOU SOW

Many times people go to the altar asking the man or woman of God to pray for their finances. But in reviewing their record of giving throughout the year, it's an embarrassment to even think about the pennies they've pitched into the offering plates. Increasing one's finances is the only thing in your life that cannot be changed solely by prayer. The Bible states it clearly: GIVE! Nonetheless, as previously mentioned, I do not advocate playing craps with God. Giving just to get and complaining about it only prevents the blessings of God.

God wants us to give out of a cheerful heart. He judges not by the phony grin on our faces, or the one-hundred-dollar bill we display for everyone to see us drop into the offering, but God judges by the intent of the heart. "Every man according as he purposeth in his heart, so let him give; not grudgingly, or of necessity: for God loveth a cheerful giver" (2 Cor. 9:7). God doesn't need our money, but He trusts us with His money. The government makes sure they take all of their taxes out of your paycheck before you get it. But God allows us to have our paychecks and from that bring to Him what rightfully belongs to Him. When we betray this trust, we curse ourselves. "You are cursed with a curse" (Mal. 3:8).

To make up for our lack, we comfort ourselves with words like, "Well, money isn't everything." And though this statement holds some truth to it, we cannot negate the fact that without money it's virtually impossible to even survive. You can't even eat without money. An overwhelming number of marriages that I counsel are in trouble simply because of a lack of money or one party's irresponsible behavior concerning money. School-age children from upper-class families sometimes take money for granted and may even tease other children who come from impoverished backgrounds, because the child's family does not have money.

The prostitute who compromises herself on the street, the drug dealer who disregards the value of other's lives, the homeless who begs for change from passersby, and the broker who rises early and stays up late—all understand the importance of money. But many times, it's those in the church who fail to understand or choose to escape the reality of the need for money and the importance of using it wisely.

Ironically, many times it's those who follow after money who consistently find themselves in debt. There must be a balance. First Timothy 6:10 states that "the love of money is the root of all evil: which while some coveted after, they have erred from the faith, and pierced themselves through with many sorrows." Many mistakenly misinterpret this scripture to mean that money is evil, but this scripture is speaking of greed. This verse should NOT be misconstrued to say that we should feel free to live our lives vicariously and without any regard for making preparations for our future and gaining control of our finances. On the other hand, you cannot love money more than you love God; you must be willing to let the money go in order to gain financial security.

Galatians 6:7–8 says that,

"whatsoever a man soweth, that shall he also reap. For he that soweth to his flesh shall of the flesh reap corruption; but he that soweth to the Spirit shall of the Spirit reap life everlasting."

So it's not only a law of physical reciprocity, but also a spiritual principle as well; you receive back into your life the things that you give out. Too many times we resort to human ingenuity to meet our needs, when God has already given us a command to seek first the kingdom of God and all these things shall then be added (Luke 12:31). This is where much of the prosperity teachings have displeased God—focusing on money and riches, but refusing to lead people to God for direction.

As a result, the pursuit of money and riches becomes more important than seeking God. God's displeasure with such behavior is made very clear. *"Ye cannot serve God and mammon"* (Matt. 6:24). When your whole mind-frame is engulfed with how to make more money and those thoughts push God aside, your greed becomes idolatry; money becomes your God. This is why we are to use wisdom in spending and learn to trust God. The gold and the silver both belong to God (Hag. 2:8), so surely He knows how to distribute it properly to meet our needs. It then becomes our responsibility, however, to avoid using His gifts negligently. So then comes the question of how to properly meet the needs, and even some of the wants, of the family.

SPIRITUAL PRINCIPLES FOR FINANCIAL FREEDOM

Unlike times past, most families today operate

from two incomes within the home. Both the husband and the wife are forced to work in order to meet the needs of the household. Because women think very differently from men and place a strong emphasis on financial stability and security, many households break up every day because the man of the house haphazardly splurges like the little boy.

The number one key to financial freedom is staying on top of your bills instead of allowing your bills to stay on top of you. Always try, as much as it is possible, to pay your bills on time. One major mistake that many men make is living day-to-day, paying past-due balances, always staying in arrears, getting deeper and deeper in debt. Bills come and even when the money is available to pay on time, temptation says, "Pay the past-due balance only and keep the rest of the money in your pocket; besides, you can always catch up next month." But when next month comes, temptation says the same thing again and again, further prolonging your debt. And the money that temptation told you to keep in your pocket...it goes down the drain to pay for insignificant "things." This is a curse!

Anytime there is enough money coming into a household to pay all the bills with some left over, yet the bills constantly stay behind, you are operating out of a generational curse that must be broken. Likewise, if you are single and working two jobs but still cannot make ends meet, you are operating out of a spirit of poverty, even though you're really not poor.

Before we show you how to break this curse, let's first identify areas of disobedience in your life and potential reasons for this curse which comes to hinder the blessings of God over your life.

1. Are You a Tither?

Tithing is not a church rule, but a commandment from God.

> "Bring ye all the tithes into the storehouse, that there may be meat in mine house, and prove me now herewith, saith the Lord of hosts, if I will not open you the windows of heaven, and pour you out a blessing, that there shall not be room enough to receive it" (Mal. 3:10).

Malachi also tells us what will happen in our disobedience to this command: "Wherein have we robbed thee? In tithes and offerings. Ye are cursed with a curse: for ye have robbed me"(Mal. 3:8–9). So it's your choice: give God His tithes and be blessed, or rob God and be cursed with a curse.

2. Do you give more time to other areas in your life than you do to God?

In their quest for riches, some of the saints of God compromise their relationship with God by showing more allegiance to a career than they do to God. Not only should you honor God with at least a tenth of your income, but also with a tenth of your time.

Don't depend on your spouse or family members to take up the slack due to your disobedience and unbelief. If you realize that you have missed the mark, it's still not too late to repair the damage that has been done. Make a commitment today to God and your family that you are working toward maturity and the ability to handle your finances wisely, and begin taking the necessary steps today.

If you feel you're in debt to the point of

irreparable damage, create a plan. Begin paying off your smaller debts first, limit your spending, and let the family know that until order has been formed in the household, many needless expenditures must stop. Don't, however, totally disregard your children's needs for recreation, clothes, and other necessities. The idea is to limit your spending and create order in the home, not chaos. Most importantly, give to God in tithes and offerings. Even the most organized plan will fail unless God is made one's first priority.

As you learn to be financially responsible, you may discover that you are your own worst enemy. In the next chapter we look at how to defeat the hidden enemies that lie within. Learn how to stop any reoccurring cycle of negative situations in your life.

10

Defeating an Enemy Called "Self"

*T*he most popular reason for ungodly behavior can oftentimes be traced back to unpleasant experiences of the past. It's usually because of these unpleasant experiences that we develop distrust, anger, anxiety, competitiveness, bitterness, and so on. And although the Book of Job reminds us that "man that is born of a woman is of few days, and full of trouble," we ignore this warning and during times of adversity embrace the attitude of helpless victim (Job 14:1). We hopelessly wallow in self-pity that only prolongs the pain and prevents recovery.

The Little Boy in Me

This is not to say, however, that we are to possess some supernatural resiliency to crises, but instead we must look at each situation as uniquely as it is presented and act upon it accordingly. "Not by might, nor by power, but by my spirit, saith the Lord of hosts" (Zech. 4:6b).

MY CRISIS INVOKES AN ANSWER

I shall never forget a time when I personally came face-to-face with a life-threatening situation that a crisis in my life presented and instantly demanded of me an answer. I was a teenager on the streets of Brooklyn, New York, confused and lawless—totally out of control. Searching for quick solutions to life-time problems, I became my own worse enemy. There was a void in my life, and I needed a quick fix—some peace—no matter how temporal. My fix became cocaine. On one particular night, I purchased the substance from the local drug dealer and resorted to my place of escape. I snorted the mixture and within minutes realized that something was drastically wrong.

The cocaine I'd purchased this particular night had been laced with embalming fluid, and this deadly mixture immediately entered my blood-stream. My heart began to palpitate fiercely. I could hear and see it pounding against my rib cage, desperately fighting to hold on to life.

Later as I lay in the emergency room, barely coherent by then, I could hear the nurse assigned to me say, "I think we have a loser on our hands." She did not mean to belittle me or imply that I was a bum. This was simply a term used to identify those who had no will to live.

Upon hearing these words uttered from her lips, it was as if the angel of the Lord immediately came down and hovered over me, relaying to me God's urgent message. And what I heard was very clear: "OK, the decision is now yours. You can live or die!" The crisis in my life was now demanding of me an answer. There was no time to ponder; my choices were clear: life or death. So, I chose life.

As a result, I am here today, alive and well by the grace of almighty God, with the ability to speak to others and let them know that they don't have to be forced into life-and-death situations because of bad decision-making or contumacious behavior. Nor do you have to allow that void in your life to needlessly be filled by man-made power when Jesus freely gives solutions and healing in every area of your life. His Word is clear: "For God sent not his Son into the world to condemn the world; but that the world through him might be saved" (John 3:17). Any time you feel the grasp of condemnation, check out the source. It's Lucifer who uses mankind to condemn, but Jesus convicts.

Destroying the Hidden Hindrances

We become our own worse enemies when we allow past traumatic experiences to breed distrust, condemnation, and other ungodly fruits, which eventually breed anger and contempt.

Distrust forces a wedge between you and those you love, further widening the void in your life. If not properly filled with healthy solutions, this void will be filled by contaminants that lead to life-threatening situations. Still, the choice is yours. Instead of viewing each obstacle as a battle where you have no option but to surrender to Lucifer, choose to look at each new trial as an opportunity to learn of the awesomeness of Jesus' power to deliver. As difficult as this sometimes may sound, learning to trust again and trusting in Jesus Christ is all that matters. Trust in Him, and truly your life will never be the same.

Trusting in Jesus alleviates the weight of disappointments caused by men. Before allowing Satan to deceive you into thinking that everyone is out to get you or that all hope is gone in your life, you must first deal with the enemy in your life called "self." Understand first, that as long as you live on this earth, oppositions will confront you, but they don't have to "take you out." It's not the magnitude of the opposition that determines the outcome, but it is how you handle the opposition, your approach, the decisions you make during opposition that determine your victory or defeat. Don't look at others as the objects of your opposition, but first look at yourself and determine, "What can I do to better myself; how can I overcome this situation; and, most importantly, how can I prevent this from happening again?"

Especially in cases where you find the same reoccurring problem, you must ask yourself, "What doors have I not closed to allow this reoccurring problem to continue entering in the same way?" For instance, I often speak to women who ask me the question, "Pastor Bloomer, it seems as if I just keep drawing to myself the same type of man—ungodly and irresponsible."

To which I kindly ask, "What residue do you still have inside of you that may keep attracting these men?"

I've said many times before, and now I'll say it again: just because a person stops doing something does not mean that he or she is delivered. Of course, it's always good to stop doing something until deliverance takes place, but we must also be wise concerning the tactics of Lucifer and his seemingly innocent devices.

If you are a woman or a man who always attracted ungodly or irresponsible persons of the opposite sex, beware. After you meet Christ and learn that these types of relationships are unhealthy for you mentally and spiritually, this new-found knowledge does not mean that you cease from being attracted to these type of individuals. Neither does it erase the fact that the other person can tell that you are attracted to him or her as well. The spirit in which you've operated for years continues to linger until deliverance comes. But there is good news. The Bible says, "Resist the devil, and he will flee from you" (James 4:7). So although you may continue to attract to yourself unhealthy relationships, unhealthy habits, and so on, you don't have to fall prey to these things. Instead, resist them until deliverance is your portion. Seek the Lord and He will reward you for your diligence.

CHANGING YOUR VIEW DETERMINES YOUR OUTCOME

People who have a negative outlook on others and take the pessimistic view in dealing with everyday issues are not in struggle with others at all. Instead they have an internal struggle within themselves— low self-esteem, lack of trust, inability to forgive, unhealed pains of the past, and so on. All of these things come for one purpose: to kill, steal, and to destroy. Inner healing must take place. Jesus came "to heal the broken-hearted, to preach deliverance to the captives...to set at liberty them that are bruised" (Luke 4:18). In other words, the battle is not yours, it's the Lord's. Your only fight is the will inside of you, which oftentimes fights you to prevent His will from being done in your life.

This fight takes place in your mind, Lucifer's greatest hideout, his place of solitude. It is in your mind where the enemy whispers to you your inevitable destruction. But you don't have to listen. The Lord will keep your mind in perfect peace when your mind is stayed on Him (Isa. 26:3). You no longer have to be the hopeless and helpless victim, degrading yourself and accepting defeat.

Early in my life as an evangelist, I found out the hard way that treating others with kindness and respect does not always guarantee a reciprocal response. There I was, a young evangelist, traveling all over the world sacrificing the needs of myself, and sometimes even those of my family, to meet the needs of others, when I realized that much of my pain was coming from those whom I loved and had helped the most.

As unbearable as the pain seemed at that time, I realized that the decision again was mine. I could shut everyone out, trust no one and extend a hand to no one again, or I could forgive. I chose the latter option, which was also the most difficult option for me at the same time. But I would not allow my destiny to be aborted by the pains I endured at the hands of those who operated in ignorance and who later would need me to minister their deliverance. I often remind my congregation that forgiveness means allowing the person to get close enough to you to do you wrong again, without allowing the individual to have free reign and rule over your life or inflict the same pain on you again.

Jesus admonishes us in Matthew 6:14-15 to forgive. He gives us the benefits of forgiveness as well as the defeat we experience when we refuse to do so:

> For if ye forgive men their trespasses, your heavenly Father will also Forgive you: But if ye forgive not men their trespasses, neither will your Father forgive your trespasses.

A very powerful example of forgiveness is shown between the relationship and commitment between David and Saul. While Saul was pursuing David unjustly, he unknowingly slipped into the same cave where David and his men were hiding. David's men admonished David that the promise of the Lord to him was being fulfilled:

> And the men of David said unto him, Behold the day of which the Lord said unto thee, Behold, I will deliver thine enemy into thine hand, that thou mayest do to him as it shall seem good unto thee (1 Sam. 24: 4).

David's response: He refused to kill Saul, as he could have, but "David arose, and cut off the skirt of Saul's robe privily" (v. 4).

Despite the fact that Saul was in pursuit to kill him, David was remorseful for having taken advantage of Saul in even this small way. "And it came to pass afterward, that David's heart smote him, because he had cut off Saul's skirt" (v. 5). David then knelt before Saul, warning him:

> Behold, this day thine eyes have seen how that the Lord had delivered thee today into mine hand in the cave: and some bade me kill thee: but mine eye spared thee; and I said, I will not put forth mine hand against my lord; for he is the Lord's anointed. Moreover, my father, see, yea, see the skirt of thy robe in my hand: for in that I cut off the skirt of thy robe, and killed thee not, know thou and see that there is neither evil nor transgression in mine hand, and I have not sinned against thee; yet thou huntest my soul to take it. The Lord judge between me and thee, and the Lord avenge me of thee: but mine hand shall not be upon thee (vv. 10-12).

In other words, David warned Saul: "The Lord delivered you into my hands, Saul, to do with you what seemed good to me to do. Some entreated me to kill you, nonetheless, I chose not to do so. In spite of our differences, you are the Lord's anointed; therefore, I will not judge you. I will allow the Lord to 'avenge me of thee,' but my hand shall not come against thee."

David understood that if he remained free of anger and contempt that the Lord would be his avenger. David understood the principles of spiritual warfare to defeat the enemy. "Not by might, nor by power, but by my spirit saith the Lord of hosts"

(Zech. 4:6). David had a revelation; man may not judge fairly, but God never fails, so allow the Lord to be the judge. "The Lord therefore be judge, and judge between me and thee, and see, and plead my cause, and deliver me out of thine hand" (1 Sam. 24:15). What else could Saul do after such an earnest declaration but admit his guilt?

> And it came to pass, when David had made an end of speaking these words unto Saul, that Saul said, Is this thy voice, my son David? And Saul lifted up his voice, and wept. And he said to David, Thou art more righteous than I: for thou hast rewarded me good, whereas I have rewarded thee evil (vv. 16–17).

Here we see that it's not the intensity of the enemy's attack that determines the outcome, but it's how David handled the situation, his ability to reason, instead of being intoxicated by anger, that allowed the continued blessings of God to permeate his life.

KNOW THE YOU INSIDE OF YOU!

Many times men allow anger to intoxicate them to the point of murder. However, you should never allow any person enough power in your life to deactivate the blessings of God and the favor of God in your life. Think before you speak, and count the cost before you react.

Know what's inside of you that's not godly— your pressure points, limitations, and boundaries. Know the proper time to react to a crisis, and know

The Little Boy in Me

the time to be silent and wait on the Lord. Embrace the principles of Ecclesiastes 3: To every thing there is a season, and a time to every purpose under the heaven: ...A time to rend, and a time to sew; a time to keep silence, and a time to speak; ...(vv. 1, 7–8).

Most importantly, defeat the enemy called self before pointing the finger or engaging in spiritual warfare on another's behalf. Remember, "the Lord's hand is not shortened, that it cannot save; neither his ear heavy, that it cannot hear" (Isa. 59:1). Though He already knows, tell Him what your problem is, and He will deliver you!

> *Dear Lord,*
>
> *No matter how much I struggle with the issue of [be honest and tell God what your issue is], I just cannot seem to break free. But today, Lord, I am sincerely and earnestly ready to be set free. Without Your help, Lord, [this issue] will continue to be a thorn in my flesh, a weakness that no matter how hard I try, I can't seem to shake. You said in Your Word that You came "to heal the broken-hearted, to preach deliverance to the captive,... recovering of sight to the blind, and to set at liberty them that are bruised." So now I surrender all to You, Lord, and ask that You deliver me and set me free! I thank You, Lord, for the miracle that You are now performing in my life as I walk in liberty and freedom in Jesus' name. Amen.*
>
> ***Warning: Only pray this prayer, if you are sincerely and honestly ready to be set free!***

11

Past, Present, Destiny

Bringing It All Together

*T*here's a little boy in every man, just as there is a little girl in every woman. The little boys and girls can be effective or ineffective. I think it's positive to be in touch with your younger side because we live in three dimensions in the earth—the past, the present, and currently approaching the future. Balance in life comes out of having a wonderful grasp on our present. Our focus on where we're going in the future is the wind that helps us sail in the present.

> Brethren, I count not myself to have apprehended: but this one thing I do, forgetting those things which are behind, and reaching forth unto those things which are

before, I press toward the mark for the prize of the high calling of God in Christ Jesus (Phil. 3:13).

GET READY FOR A GREAT COMEBACK

Knowing God means that you are going to have to acquaint yourself with the greatest comeback ever. In other words, you are going to embrace resurrection power. Knowing God also means that the enemy wants to take you out. Certainly he's tried to take me out on several occasions. After a short time, however, I got wise enough to realize that even if I went down, I would come up again! And every time I would come back up, I always arose with more strength, more power, and more revelation. My battle cry became, "You can try to take me out if you want to, devil, but I will come back again."

Remember, praise is your greatest defense. Don't ever underestimate the power of your own personal praise. True, it is wonderful to have others pray for you, but don't ever underestimate the power of your own personal praise. In many instances, we mistakenly run around "bumming" prayers like borrowing a cup of sugar from the neighbor next door when deliverance can usually be found in one's praise.

Praise is your tool of resurrection. Regardless of the situation, if you start praising God, a shift takes place. For instance, you can't praise God and remain sad all day long; you can't praise God and remain angry or jealous. Praise changes your situation, so if you want your situation changed, then praise Him!

That I may know him, and the power of

his resurrection, and the fellowship of his sufferings, being made comformable unto his death (Phil. 3:10).

So knowing Christ means that you not only acquaint yourself with great comebacks, but you also have to acquaint yourself with seasons of suffering. And this is the part of the text that most people hate to address or even consider. The fact is that great ministries are born out of suffering and great marriages are purged through suffering. Suffering produces a cohesiveness that is second to none; thus, great relationships are made out of suffering. "If we suffer [with Him]," the Bible says, then "we shall also reign with Him" (2 Tim. 2:12). So no one occupies the lofty places of ministry without suffering. No one experiences the great blessings of the Lord, nor develops great relationships, without suffering.

THREE DIMENSIONS: MY PAST, MY PRESENT, MY FUTURE

Philippians 3:13–14 describes what we are to do with the three dimensions of time in our lives.

The Past—Forgetting those things which are behind.
The Present—Reaching forth unto those things which are before.
The Future—Press toward the mark for the prize of the high calling of God in Christ Jesus.

We know that the battle is not ours, but it belongs

135

to the Lord. Weeping may endure for a night, but joy comes in the morning (Ps. 30:5). In spite of our pasts, we must make up our minds to reach toward those things that God has in store; we must press toward the mark in order to receive the prize of the higher calling. In Philippians 3, Paul deals with the three dimensional stages of the human being. Not only are we body, soul, and spirit, but we live in three separate time dimensions. We all have a past, we live in the present, and we're trying to embrace the future.

The text, then, is powerful because what Paul is trying to convey is, "It's not all of my education that has brought me to this natural understanding concerning my three dimensional stages and the importance of endurance. But instead it's my ability to prevent my past from beating up my present in such a violent way that it causes me to become stagnated, thus placing me in somewhat of a holding pattern and making it impossible for me to land or to move. I will not allow my past to destroy my future!"

So Paul says, "Brethren, I count not myself to have apprehended, but this one thing I do, forgetting those things which are behind, I reach forth to the things which are before me and then I place myself in the press" (Phil. 3:13–14, paraphrased).

In one of his visions in the Book of Revelation, John saw a great ocean. An angel explained to him that "*The waters which thou sawest* are peoples, and multitudes, and nations, and tongues" (Rev. 17:15, italics added). This metaphor helped me to see a parable about life today.

In my parable, your life is a boat that is placed in the sea of people. Your boat (your life) does not have an engine. It does not have jet power or a propeller. The only power to move your boat is a paddle or wind that blows. Therefore, it's your sail that controls your destiny. Your sail, your standard that you send up, is propelled by the winds of your past, the winds of your present, and the winds of your future.

Did you catch that? The power is in the wind. Now in understanding that, if the wind of your past blows from behind you, then it is pushing you into your present and into your future, and you'll reach your destination. Your destiny is secure. But if the wind from your past is contrary, flips around, and blows from ahead instead of pushing you from behind, you go backward, further away from your destination. The contrary winds of your past will stall your present boat and force you to live in the past, and living in the past aborts your spiritual destiny.

Living in the past is a major problem for many of us. Although it's important to remember where you come from in order to have a clear understanding of what you're going through, you can't allow your past to constantly push your boat back to where you come from.

The devil's goal is to take your natural mind and force it to remember your past, and your past says, *You can't do it.* In reality, what is holding you back is not your neighbor. It's not your mother who offended you, nor your daddy or uncle who abused you. It's none of those things. Now it's just you and your past fears making it impossible for you to enjoy this season of peace in your present reign. Consequently, you're constantly occupying the past and carrying everybody back there with you, even people you don't even know. Every time you open up your mouth, you're talking about your abuse, complaining and transferring your anguish into others instead of testifying of the marvelous power of the Almighty to deliver and set free.

The Bible is clear: "[Cast] down imaginations, and every high thing that exalteth itself against the knowledge of God" (2 Cor. 10:5). Remember, the knowledge of God is a spirit. It is not human knowledge. When demons come to you and place vain imaginations in your mind, the imaginations are so powerful that they can totally remove the plan of God from your mind. These vain thoughts are so powerful that they exalt themselves above the knowledge of God.

Remember, God began planning your life before you were even flesh and blood, before you were even an embryo in your mother's womb. He says in the book of Jeremiah, "Before I formed thee in the belly I knew thee; and before thou camest forth out of the womb I sanctified thee" (Jer. 1:5). You did not come from your mother and father, you came from God—from heaven—and God has released you into the earth with a set purpose and a set destiny. But it's up to you to reach it.

For we know that if God is who He says He is (and He is), then He'll do exactly what He said He would do. He always does. That means that every person He creates and releases into this unfinished world is a finished product. This is evidenced by the text that says He's the "author and the finisher of our faith" (Heb. 12:2).

Your faith is completed in Christ before He you even accept Christ. You did not find God. Get that out of your head. Neither did God have to find you.

Why? Because He created you. He formed you and placed you in the earth to produce certain things. Ephesians 1 says, "Blessed be the God and Father of our Lord Jesus Christ, who hath blessed us with all spiritual blessings in heavenly places in Christ...as he hath chosen us in him before the foundation of the world"(Eph. 1:3-4). This is a foundational plan that God put together before the world was ever even brought into existence.

While I do understand that many of us have gone through many different types of abuse and other issues, I also believe that the Lord sometimes removes things from us for a certain season until we're strong enough to deal with them. Allowing other people to determine your greatness, trying to get someone to confirm your greatness, and looking for confirmation and affirmation from individuals who have not experienced what you've experienced is a needless waste of time.

It's wonderful to have a great philosophy; it's wonderful to know numerous scholars; it's wonderful to have a whole lot of books, but experience is truly the best teacher. God does not sit down and mass-produce snowflakes, but every snowflake that falls is significantly different. Likewise, God does not mass-produce man either. Every one of us has a different DNA pattern. Newborn babies are not born with dead people's fingerprints. God does not run out of a pattern or an order, so stop boxing God in, stop trying to be like someone else, and get your own vision for your own destiny.

Forget those things which are behind, and reach forth to the things which are before—the present— and then press. Your past propels you into the present, and the present is now propelling you into

The Little Boy in Me

your future. Know that you have purpose and destiny on board, and the days of just coming to church to hear another sermon are long gone.

GROW UP MY CHILD

I wrote a very popular song about the potential of the little boy whose youth was robbed from him. The words seem to sum up the matter concerning destiny:

> Grow up, my child, it's time to come out
>   but not to play.
> Grow up, my child, the little boy in you—
>   don't let him rot away.
> You could be a genius, president,
>   preacher, or movie star.
> The pains were for your making,
> And the scars to remind you of who you
>   are.
> Grow up, my child.

The truth of the matter is, there's a little boy or girl in every one of us. When I was a little boy, I was forced to be a man and when I became a man, I turned out to be a little boy. This was due to a number of experiences that happened in my life to steer this drastic change. At ages nine and ten, I was spending my time in front of the Empire State Building in New York, shining shoes for fifteen cents, stealing newspapers off the back of the daily newspaper truck and selling them in order to carry money home to my mother because Daddy was not there.

So there I was, a little boy taking on very adult

responsibilities. But as I grew older, the little boy inside of me began coming out. Some people are too young to be as serious as they are, and others are too old to be as silly as they are. There must be a balance, otherwise the age that you've missed will catch you at the most inopportune time.

I remember when I was little, my sister, who was the oldest child at home at the time, ran away when she was about thirteen years old. She ran away because my mother had nine children, and by the time my sister was nine years old she was cooking and cleaning and taking care of all of the younger siblings. My mother was not around much during this time, so my sister was forced to take on very adult-like responsibilities.

Needless to say, the first opportunity that she got to get away from her environment, she fled. We would not see or hear from her again until she was about eighteen years old. When she did show up, my sister was with child. The remainder of her life was lived in torment, anguish, and bitterness over the things she endured as a little girl. Her childhood was interrupted, and she unfortunately filled the void with drugs. She now suffers a terminal illness, placing her life at a standstill, ceasing any hope for future growth without divine intervention of the Lord Jesus Christ.

MY ABUSE

My mother had nine children by my father, who then went outside of the wedding bond and had approximately fifteen other children by six different women. I never remember my father living in the household with us, only that he would come periodically to discipline us: knock us around, stomp us, punch us, and whip us.

In spite of the abuse, however, I loved my father, for a long time. It wasn't the abuse he inflicted on me that at last caused me to stop loving him so much. Instead, it was the abuse that he inflicted on my mother. It wasn't enough that he abused her inside the home, but he wanted to embarrass her as well. So on one particular night he shoved her out of the door into the hallway of the projects where we lived and began beating her in the presence of others. And when the judge ordered him never to touch my mother again, he'd wrap his hands in towels so that the bruises on his hands would not betray him and still inflict his blows with brute force.

The reason I'm a protector of women today is because of the aggressions of my father against my mother. I am without a doubt a protector of women. In spite of the abuse, my life now is a testament of the healing power of God, His ability to set the captives free and turn what the devil meant for bad around for our good. If I allowed my abusive past to dictate my future, not only would my church not grow, but I probably would not even be a pastor at this time. In spite of my past, the Lord has created for me a wonderful future and is now propelling me into my future.

Age Nine & CEO

I feel that even at a very young age, God had already placed within my mindset to be very business-minded. As a child I always had a plan, an idea, something to do. For example, under the projects where I lived as a child there was a basement. In order to access the basement, you had to go down a ramp, so everybody called the basement "the ramp." The ramp was where all the trash was thrown and where the garbage trucks came to retrieve it. I remember on one particular afternoon someone had thrown a very nice desk into the ramp. Upon noticing the desk I immediately had an idea: this would be my desk, a place for me to carry out my day-to-day "business" activities. So there I was, nine years old, sweating to get the desk out of the ramp, into the elevator and into the apartment.

Some time later I found a black leather chair that someone had thrown out, and, although it wasn't an office chair, it was a "big" chair. There were no legs on their chair and it needed much repair, but I, the young CEO of my own imaginary company, had yet another grand idea. I brought the chair upstairs and placed it on top of a smaller chair that I'd retrieved from school, thus making for myself a business-like chair. Fortunately, by this time my brothers and sisters were getting older and they were starting to move out, which allowed me to have my own room. So there in the back of my bedroom was this big chair. And there I was in this big chair with my desk.

So my ministry or my businesses didn't start when I became an adult, but they all started as a dream for me as a child. I've always envisioned great things. In my overall mindset, I started pastoring a church between the ages of nine and eleven years old. I didn't know I was a preacher, nor did I even know that I was called. But I was always business-minded and never without a plan. I wasn't destined for jail, as some tried to coerce me into believing. Although I did spend time in jail, I knew that wasn't my destiny.

Instead, what I'm doing now—pastoring, evangelizing, being used of God to change people's lives—that is my destiny. As a youth I would use cardboard boxes as my pulpit, and when we went to the Seventh-Day Adventist Church, although they preached very quietly, I was always yelling and clapping my hands. Although I wasn't from a Pentecostal background, the fire of God was always in me!

MY DESK AND MY CHAIR

The housing authority told my mother that because all of the kids had moved out with the exception of my sister, Crystal, my brother, Zachary, and me that we'd have to move into a smaller apartment. So my mother chose to move into apartment C, which had two bedrooms. This meant that my brother and me had to now share a bedroom, while my sister would either share the other room with my mother or sleep in the living room on the couch. (She chose the couch.) Of course, this drastic move of condensing from three apartments into one caused mixed feelings and emotions. But it wasn't that we would no longer be living in the "penthouse in the projects" that bothered me. What caused me great concern was, "What am I going to do with my desk and my chair?"

Though seemingly insignificant, this desk and chair had become my only means of reminding myself of what the future could hold—my escape, my destiny. It was my symbol of freedom. God always shows you your destiny, your end, at your beginning. If you listen to the stories of great men and women today, many of their stories are all the same. They will tell you how it took them years to learn that what happened in their pasts actually had meaning to something that would later unfold in their futures.

So, returning to my desk story, the top of it was covered with insignificant little trinkets and other items that meant nothing to anybody, but my greatest concern was that my destiny was now in jeopardy. I didn't care about my bed or anything else, only my desk—my destiny, my promise, my goal. So when my mother informed us that we would have to condense our belongings in order to move, my heart went into my stomach. While standing in the kitchen with her one day, I wanted so desperately to ask her, "What about my desk and my chair?" but I just couldn't bring myself to do it.

The day that we moved into the smaller apartment, I was in school. When I came home all the furniture was moved, the apartment in disarray, *stuff* everywhere. I didn't say a word. My mother was standing in the kitchen, and she said to me, "It's gonna be tight in here" [meaning the apartment]. As I scanned the living room, I saw furniture and other items, but no desk.

My heart began beating with unrelenting force; I was so afraid that I could feel butterflies in my stomach. I walked past the kitchen to what would be my new bedroom. Too afraid to ask, but hoping it was there, I entered the room, and right next to the bed, over in the corner, there it was—my desk and my chair! I turned with exhilaration and ran back to the kitchen. Before I could say a word, my mother responded, "I got your desk," with a parental smile of protection, knowing she had met the need of her child, knowing within herself that what was trash to everyone else was her son's greatest treasure. That incident endeared my mother to me, and somehow all of the other transgressions that she committed suddenly lost significance in comparison to the fact that my mother had done this just for me.

I think that we can all tell stories from our past that can help others to better understand why we behave the way we do, who we really are, our weaknesses, and our strengths. Many of my stories help the people who are closest to me understand why I take such a strong stand against some things, and why in other areas I'm very compassionate.

Sometimes, in choir rehearsal at my church, for instance, I may feel very serious about interrupting rehearsal and sharing a new idea. But because they perform all the songs that particular night so well and everything moves smoothly I don't say in a serious tone, "Let's take a break." I create a break instead. I might do something as silly as placing fake teeth in my mouth and standing in front of them while they're singing, causing uncontrollable laughter because they need it, not me. They have served me well. They've given their all to me and I have to give back to them. The little-boy quality about me allows me to do that.

Many of you in reading this book are remembering a number of defining points that took place in your life. From the time your dad took you to a ball game, to your mother buying those sneakers you always wanted, and other powerful things that happened to shape your life and force you to grow up. You may be remembering your desk and your chair that was not moved but was left behind. Now you're struggling with the mere fact that there was no room for your desk and your chair, or whatever it was that you used as your route of escape. Nonetheless, life continues to needlessly pass you by.

Regardless of what was left behind, you must now press toward the future that God still has in store for you. Sometimes who you are destined to be in the future, you already are in the present, even though the natural manifestation of that great person may not recognized or affirmed by man. I believe that much of my success as owner of a record company and publishing house, as a national speaker, Bible teacher, pastor, and successful businessman comes out of experience that started when I was nine years old, growing up in the projects. Amidst all the pain and suffering, here was a defining moment where my mother took time to find room for my desk.

I think that many of us are harboring bitterness because of situations in our past that made it impossible for one of our parents to engage in activities with us due to over crowding in the home, or because they were too preoccupied with other issues. Now has come the time, however, to allow such hindrances to flee and no longer be a part of our daily conversations and complaints. Remember these things only as a testament to the power of God, His love and mercy that He had for you, which allowed you to endure.

Now ask yourself, Are you truly ready to be set free? Would you like to experience what it feels like to finally walk in victory and freedom? If the answer is yes, then let us agree together that the bonds of Lucifer will no longer hold you captive to your past. Amen.